# INSPIRED TRAVELLER'S GUIDE
## HIDDEN PLACES

# INSPIRED TRAVELLER'S GUIDE

## HIDDEN PLACES

SARAH BAXTER

ILLUSTRATIONS BY
AMY GRIMES

WHITE LION
PUBLISHING

Brimming with creative inspiration, how-to projects and useful information to enrich your everyday life, Quarto Knows is a favourite destination for those pursuing their interests and passions. Visit our site and dig deeper with our books into your area of interest: Quarto Creates, Quarto Cooks, Quarto Homes, Quarto Lives, Quarto Drives, Quarto Explores, Quarto Gifts, or Quarto Kids.

First published in 2020 by White Lion Publishing,
an imprint of The Quarto Group.
The Old Brewery, 6 Blundell Street,
London, N7 9BH,
United Kingdom
T (0)20 7700 6700
www.QuartoKnows.com

© 2020 Quarto Publishing plc.
Illustration copyright © 2020 by Amy Grimes

Every effort has been made to trace the copyright holders of material quoted in this book. If application is made in writing to the publisher, any omissions will be included in future editions.

A catalogue record for this book is available from the British Library.

ISBN  978 1 78131 920 8
Ebook ISBN 978 1 78131 921 5

10 9 8 7 6 5 4 3 2 1

Design by Paileen Currie

Printed in China

# CONTENTS

| INTRODUCTION | WHAT DOES 'hidden' actually mean? Secret, out of sight, undercover? Secluded and tucked away? Camouflaged, cryptic, mysterious, arcane? Hidden is all these things and more – a hidden place is one |
| --- | --- |

that confers a feeling that you're somehow peeling back a layer, going somewhere few have been, gaining an insight into something once – or still – concealed.

That's the premise behind this uncloaking compendium. It's not a comprehensive guide, but a glimpse beneath the covers of a few of the planet's part-obscured places. Sites with stories to disclose; sites of majesty and mystery that have provided shelter, inspiration, strategic advantage and spiritual succour to our ancestors across the ages.

This book uncovers a selection of hidden spots. Maybe some you've never heard of; some you have; some that are on your radar but perhaps whose story you don't quite know. The aim is to lift the lid a little to bring their stories to the fore; to encourage exploration beyond the more obvious places to these secret repositories of wonder and intrigue instead. In this, your armchair travel is aided by beautiful illustrations, which help evoke the aura of each locale, helping every entry to live on the page.

So yes, there are many types of hidden. For starters, some spots are concealed by virtue of their location – they're unreachable by road, adrift in hostile deserts, teetering on mountaintops or sunk at the bottom of the sea. And the effort to get to them only enhances the joy of discovery. For instance, there are a thousand – tens of thousands – of valleys in the Alps, where geranium-bright chalets nestle prettily between the mountains. So what makes the Kaisertal (page 42) any better? It's the heightened spirit of adventure required to reach it, and the knowledge that the people who still live here – whose ancestors have done so for centuries – have different tales to tell.

Then there are places that are physically concealed, maybe shrouded in a pelage of greenery, an insinuation of tree roots, a dusting of dirt and sand, an almost all consuming jungle. Human history being steadily or rampantly reclaimed by nature so that its original meaning has become obscured. Places once grand and powerful now poking timidly from behind shrubbery and scrubbery, moss and weeds. Such places include Cambodia's ruinous Phnom Kulen (page 86), the first capital of the Khmer Empire, which once ruled swathes of Southeast Asia. Now it sits almost forgotten atop its overgrown plateau, its true identity only confirmed to the world in the past decade. This fallen great is almost within touching distance of the magnificent temple complex of Angkor – the site that usurped Phnom Kulen, and that sees over 2.5 million visitors a year. But no more than a trickle of those hordes make the detour to uncover the buried treasure nearby.

And that's key. So many hidden sites offer a more intimate travel experience. Because they might be harder to reach, lesser known or off-grid, they offer something special to those who make the effort to seek them. The chance to walk amid past stories without the whirr of the present; to uncover their secrets without having to push through the crowds; the chance to view, to touch, to understand something that maybe few others have ever seen. To seek out a hidden place is to opt for the path less taken, to expand your mind. Which seems the true spirit of travel. As once said by unconventional adventuress Mary Schäffer Warren – whom you'll meet by Maligne Lake on page 106 – 'I hate doing the ordinary thing'.

Sometimes it's less the site that is hidden than its meaning. The bricks and mortar, the architecture and artistry, are in plain view, but the story has been skewed, by memory or even malice. Take Great Zimbabwe (page 76), a ruined city that is the finest ancient construction in Africa south of the Sahara Desert. It's quite remote, a good half-day's drive from Harare. And weeds frill the cracks in its venerable walls. But the 'hidden' theme here concerns the truth. For years Zimbabwe's colonial masters muddied the origins of this significant site, spinning a fiction that suited their prejudice and agenda, keeping Great Zimbabwe's actual origins veiled from the people whose ancestors were behind its creation. To know this as you wander around its expert-made ramparts is to see it with completely different eyes.

There are many more places that could have been revealed on these pages. Perhaps we could have taken a hot hike through the tropics to reach Ciudad Perdida, Colombia's 'lost city', built by the Tairona people around 1,200 years ago and now sunken back into the jungle. Or we could have delved into Derinkuyu, the labyrinthine underground city carved into the soft tuff of Cappadocia in Turkey, where early Christians hid out to avoid religious persecution. Or perhaps we could have sailed to the 'Forbidden Island' of Ni'ihau, a tiny, long-off-limits isle that is one of the last bastions of traditional Hawaiian culture; now, small numbers of visitors are permitted on guided tours.

Or maybe the next best place that could have been included in these pages hasn't even been rediscovered. With the tendency of both human brains and Mother Nature to erode, cover over, misremember and forget, who knows what sites and stories we're yet to find?

## TYNEHAM

THERE ARE no parcels piled up in the post office these days; no jars of liquorice on the counter nor sounds of telegrams being relayed from the back room. No coats hang off the hooks in the school hall. The terraced cottages, once quaintly thatched, lie ruined and roofless; their walls bare, their fireplaces cold and empty. Tucked into the folds of the Purbeck Hills, in earshot of the English Channel, this solemn little village has lost its villagers. Or rather, they've lost it. The Taylors and the Tizzards, the Wares and the Wheelers, the Balsons, Brachis and Bonds – families of another time and, now, another place. Evicted 'temporarily' for the sake of the greater good, never to return ...

On 17 November 1943, deep into World War II, Major-General Miller at the British War Department sent each resident of Tyneham a letter. It told of the urgent need for civilian-free land on which troops could train. Unfortunately Tyneham was just the ticket. 'It is regretted,' the Major-General wrote, 'that, in the National Interest, it is necessary to move you from your homes.' The letter concludes: 'The Government appreciate that this is no small sacrifice ... but they are sure that you will give this further help towards winning the war with a good heart.'

The village of Tyneham is said to date back to the Iron Age; it was mentioned in the 1086 Domesday Book (known then as 'Tigeham', or 'goat enclosure') and later had a fine three-storey Elizabethan manor, considered one of the finest houses in Dorset. But all that counted for nought in 1943, when the 250 or so inhabitants were given just 30 days to pack up and leave.

With preparations for the Allied invasion of Normandy (D-Day) progressing apace, the military requisitioned the village and 3,035 hectares (7,500 acres) of surrounding chalk down and heathland for their secret training operations. Tyneham was, unluckily, close to Lulworth Camp, which had long been used as a tank firing range. As World War II dragged on, and more powerful weapons began to be developed, the Lulworth range was deemed insufficient. So the adjacent areas – including tiny Tyneham – were commandeered.

The villagers left in good faith, believing they would be permitted to return at the war's end. They left a note tacked to the church door: 'Please treat the church and houses with care. We have given up our homes where many of us have lived for generations, to help win the war to keep men free. We shall return one day and thank you for treating the village kindly.'

But that promise was broken. After the war, with memories of atrocities still fresh and the Cold War brewing, the army deemed it necessary to hold on to this useful training ground. Because most of the residents were tenants, the only compensation they received was the rough valuation of the produce in their gardens.

Despite various protests, the Ministry of Defence has remained steadfast. None of the former residents – not Reverend Friend nor post mistress Gwendoline Driscoll, not even the Bonds, whose family had owned the manor since 1683 – has ever been able to return to live in their homes.

However, it is possible for anyone to pay a visit. Although the Lulworth ranges are still used for live firing exercises, for up to 150 days a year – usually weekends and public holidays – the guns stop, the white flags fly and members of the public are allowed to access Tyneham, to stroll through a village that's part time capsule, part wreckage of war, despite being so far from the frontline.

The Church of Saint Mary the Virgin, which originally dates to the 13th century, has fared best. It fell into ruin after the villagers left, and some of its interior fittings – such as the bells, organ and Jacobean pulpit – were relocated, but the structure has been repaired. The church is now a small museum telling the story of Tyneham; the names of the displaced villagers line the walls. Outside, it's possible to see the few residents who have made it back home: with special permission from the military, some have been buried in the graveyard.

Also still standing is the one-room school, though its own fate was sealed well before that of the rest of Tyneham. Built to educate 60 children, who walked in from surrounding farms, the number of students had fallen to only nine by 1932, so the school was forced to close. Now, however, it's fully restored, its wooden benches, dog-eared books, chalkboard and cane suggesting a lesson is about to start.

Less fortunate was the Elizabethan manor. By the time the valley was evacuated in 1943, it had already been requisitioned by the Royal Air Force. Over the subsequent years its most valuable features were stripped out, including stone porchways, wood panels and glassware; eventually it was demolished by the army. The rubble lies a little outside the village, tucked into Tyneham's Great Wood, always off-limits.

However, most of Tyneham's tattered houses are open for viewing. The cottages of the main street, Post Office Row, are without roofs and floors – though have been made structurally safe. There are no street lamps, no electricity poles, no water pipes, no signs of the passing of the last century – except, perhaps, for the public telephone box, installed in 1929. It's no longer connected, of course, but some say you occasionally hear it ring, a melancholy call to no one in this village of ghosts ...

| Where? | Orkney, Scotland |
|---|---|
| What? | Neolithic relic, preserved under sand, threatened by the sea |

## SKARA BRAE

THE BLUE waves and soft-blonde sand of the Bay of Skaill sneak almost right up to the ancient stones of Skara Brae. But it wasn't always this way. When the first inhabitants staked their claim to this remote outpost of Scotland – before the Egyptians built the Pyramids, before the erection of Stonehenge – theirs was an inland village, by the side of a freshwater loch. But time and tides have tinkered with this landscape, reshaping the shoreline, advancing the dunes and eventually interring the village itself. Like a Pompeii without the pyroclastics, Skara Brae lay long buried, waiting for a time when it might rise again to reveal the secrets of the past ...

The Neolithic village of Skara Brae is thought to have been built around 3200 BC, when it was home to a small community of hunters, fishermen and pioneering farmers – some of Britain's first-ever agriculturalists. Abandoned some 600 years later, for reasons unknown, the village remains were left to survive the wild Orkney elements alone. And survive they did. Over the centuries, the site was buried under a drifting wall of sand that ultimately safeguarded what lay beneath. The result of this mummification by Mother Nature? Skara Brae is one of the best-preserved Neolithic settlements in Western Europe.

Mother Nature finally decided to lay bare the site in the winter of 1850. A violent storm hit the island, and the particular combination of whipping winds and exceptionally high tides blasted away the veil of dirt and grasses. The sand mound that locals had come to know as 'Skerrabra' turned out to be something rather more significant.

Following the storm, William Watt, seventh Laird of Skaill House – a grand 17th-century manor, right by Skara Brae – noticed the outlines of buildings emerging from the sand. Watt proceeded to spend several years excavating the site; the remains of four ancient dwellings were initially discovered as well as many artefacts. So rich was the bounty that he set up a private museum in what's now Skaill House's dining room.

In the 1920s another storm and further excavations disclosed more of the village's secrets; in total, nine houses were unearthed. At this time Skara Brae was still believed to be an Iron Age settlement, dating from around 500 BC. It wasn't until the site was radiocarbon-dated in the 1970s that its true, venerable age was confirmed.

Skara Brae is no longer hidden. A wall has been built in an attempt to stall the rising seas; the visitor path around the ruins is well trodden; cruise ships often disgorge large gaggles of tourists. But despite the fact that this long-concealed site is now so blatantly on show, a visit still feels like a trip back 5,000 years. The scatter of circular stone-slab houses sits much as it always has. Each was set into large midden heaps (the piled rubbish provided much-needed insulation) and connected to the others by covered passageways. They no longer have roofs – it's believed they were once topped with turf, skins or thatched seaweed – but they do still have furniture. Each single-room dwelling has a central hearth that is flanked by stone beds (once likely softened by heather mattresses); shelved stone dressers face the main entrance. There are no windows, but there is a drainage system, and evidence that suggests a primitive sort of indoor toilet. So far, so relatively comfortable.

But the residents of Skara Brae weren't merely subsisting. Finds such as necklaces and pendants, richly carved objects, pottery and dice paint a picture of a creative people who liked to make things for pleasure, who enjoyed a game or two. Walking around the tidy mounds and the displays of treasures, personalities begin to emerge from the silent stone, and an ancient era becomes that little bit clearer for the modern mind to grasp.

## MENLO CASTLE

LIKE STARING at a *Magic Eye* picture, you can't see it until you *see it*. At first there looks to be nothing but a fuzz of foliage; a tangle of leaves, vines and trees clumped by the riverbank. But concentrate harder, and the cloak of invisibility begins to lift. There's substance behind that choke of green. The leafage leaps into man-made forms: gables and chimney stacks, window holes and crenellations. As rooks caw up above and the waterway gently burbles, a castle takes shape. A once magnificent manor beset by tragedy, now being swallowed by Mother Nature ...

'Of all the countries in the world, Ireland is the country for ruins.' So noted German writer and geographer Johann Georg Kohl after travelling there in 1841. 'Here you have ruins of every period ... each century has marked its progress.' Certainly Ireland is replete with ailing castles. A history plagued by conflict means the country was moved to create an abundance of these defensive structures, which were ritually destroyed by invading forces or rival clans. Many castles fell to the New Model Army during the 17th-century Cromwellian conquest; others were firebombed in the early 20th century, during the Irish War of Independence. The prevailing weather – Atlantic-blown, notoriously damp – has speeded the deterioration of some; others have been victims of poor economics or bad luck.

One such victim of the latter is half-hidden Menlo. Built on the River Corrib in 1569, it was the ancestral home of the Blakes, one of the 14 Tribes of Galway – the families that dominated politics and trade in medieval Galway – and once the richest and most

influential family in the county. Sir Thomas Blake was Mayor of Galway at the time the castle was constructed, and many of his descendants went on to hold the same post. In 1651, Sir Thomas's great-great-grandson, Sir Valentine, fought for the Royalists against Cromwell during the Siege of Galway, and his failure to defend the town saw him stripped of his property. However, thanks to brother Walter, a wealthy wine and wool merchant, Menlo Castle was saved. And it continued to house the Blakes until 26 July 1910, when disaster struck.

Reports called it the worst fire in the west of Ireland for decades. No one knows how it began but it's thought to have started in the apartment of Miss Ellen Blake, invalid daughter of the then baronet, who was resident at the time. The alarm was raised around 5.40a.m. The coachman managed to escape by climbing out of his window. The household's only other residents, two servant girls, were trapped on the roof and had to jump; one died. By the time the fire brigade arrived, it was too late. The whole building was alight and raging. By 7a.m., the roof had collapsed and the insides had been gutted. Miss Ellen's body was never found. The castle has been a ruin ever since.

Some say Menlo is the handsomest of all Ireland's abandoned keeps. It's arguably the most concealed. The castle hides in plain sight, just a few miles outside Galway, its pelisse of weeds and ivy so completely swamping the old stone walls that they merge right into the fields. From the University of Galway, on the opposite side of the river, you have to squint to make it out at all.

Get closer, approaching via Menlo cemetery – where several Blakes have been laid to rest – and you'll see a drive leading under an old stone arch. Beyond this, a rusty gate and gangs of nettles are all the defences the castle mounts these days. Officially, this is private land, but many a curious passerby has vaulted the gate for a closer look. Valuable paintings and rich Belgian tapestries, said to be 300 years old, went up in the blaze, as did the whole interior. All that remains are doorless doorways, empty fireplaces and hints in the masonry of Menlo's distinguished past.

| Where? | Funen, Denmark |
|---|---|
| What? | Buried Viking boat that once carried a king |

## LADBY SHIP

HE MUST have been distinguished indeed, to be buried in such style. No coffin carried this Viking chieftain into the afterlife. For him, a great warship – almost the length of a blue whale – served as a sarcophagus, with a wealth of treasures for his final voyage stashed inside: food and drink, jewellery and weapons, sacrificial dogs and horses. The send-off would have been spectacular: a lengthy bacchanal of feasting and chanting, dancing and trances, maybe sacrifices, suicides, sex. And then, the whole precious pyre would have been set alight, sending a thick plume of smoke swirling skyward, lifting the nobleman's spirit into the next realm, while the charred remains were piled with soil, raising a mound to his memory to last for centuries ...

For Vikings, those greatest of medieval travellers, the most significant journey of all was the last – the journey into the hereafter. To be buried in the proper way was to give the deceased the smoothest passing into either the hallowed realms of Valhalla (for the bravest warriors) or Helgafjell (for non-warriors who'd lived a good life). All Norsemen and women would be interred with their key possessions and then cremated to release their ashes directly into the heavens. But for those of highest rank, the rituals would be all the more elaborate. Such as at the ship burial of Ladby.

There are other Viking ship burials across the Norse world; many are more impressive, with fine vessels that are displayed in high-tech museums. But the one discovered near the small town of Kerteminde in 1935 is the only such site to be have been found in

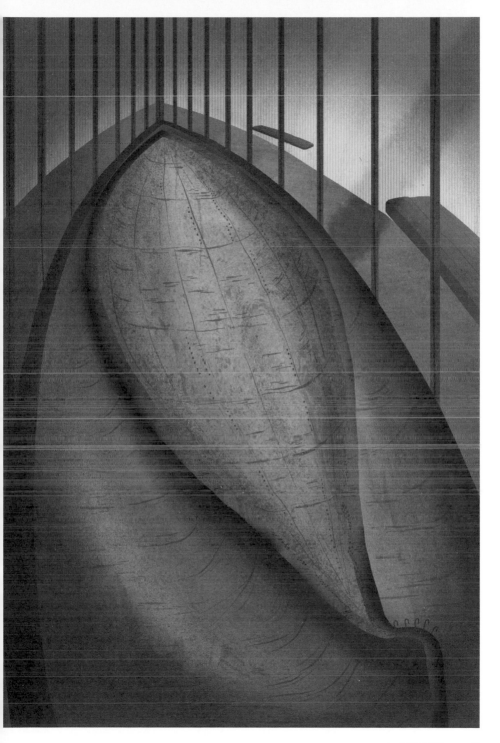

Denmark, and it is the only such site where the ship – or at least what's left of it – can be viewed exactly where it was placed, over 1,000 years ago.

Ship burials are commonly found on higher ground, near water. The Ladby ship is true to form, located atop a rise by the shores of Kerteminde Fjord. In around AD 925, following the death of the King of Ladby, the ruler's wooden ship was hauled from the water, probably with the aid of rollers, to form his tomb. Little is left of the boat, its wooden planks long since rotten away. But its outline remains imprinted in the earth, the shadow of a longship measuring 21.5 metres (70.5 feet) long and 3 metres (10 feet) wide, built to seat around 30 rowers and equipped with mast and sail. It was possibly brightly painted, as during the original excavation traces of yellow and blue pigment were found. The prow is shaped like a dragon's head, the aft like a dragon's tail, both with manes of decorative iron curls. Other pieces of metalwork have survived, including the original anchor and chain, the rings for the rigging and around 2,000 rivets, which indicate where the decayed planks once sat.

No Viking would be buried without their grave goods – the provisions for the afterlife that would indicate their earthly status. In the belly of the boat lie the teeth and bones of at least 11 horses as well as several dogs, which would have been slaughtered before being placed by the king. Some 600 objects were uncovered during the excavation, including a silver belt buckle, a gilded dog lead, a bronze platter, stirrups and spurs, and some kind of board game. Unfortunately, the grave appears to have been plundered at some point, with precious items stolen and the chieftain's remains mutilated – perhaps the work of a rival clan seeking to assert their own might.

Now, the remaining treasures can be seen in a small museum, along with a reconstruction of the burial showing the chieftain laid out in a full-scale replica, surrounded by his grave goods. The ship itself remains in situ, now beneath a mound of concrete rather than earth and grass. And though rotten and crumbling, it still speaks across the centuries, an enduring symbol of Viking power.

## OUR DEAR LORD IN THE ATTIC

FROM THE outside this townhouse on the Oudezijds Voorburgwal canal looks little different to any other. Handsome, yes, in Dutch Golden Age style, its proportions tall and slender, its facade crowned by a soaring spout gable. But of more note is what lies within. Above the old kitchen and the day rooms, along the narrow corridors, up the steep, creaking stairs, right at the top: a church. Unexpectedly tucked into the attic is a place of worship, with a Baroque altar, a painting of the baptism of Christ, sculptures of the apostles, a made-to-fit organ. This secret chapel is a symbol of hidden faith, and a lesson on past tolerance that well befits the present day ...

Ons' Lieve Heer op Solder (Our Dear Lord in the Attic), and the house in which it rests, was built in the 17th century, at a time of both Dutch dominance and division. In July 1581, seven northerly United Provinces – the precursor of the modern-day Netherlands – declared their independence from the Spanish king, shifting the fledgling nation from majority Catholic to Protestant; in a subsequent declaration, the overt practice of Catholicism was banned. But many people remained loyal to their former faith, secretly celebrating mass in their homes or workplaces – or even constructing their own churches.

Such was the case for Jan Hartman, a successful Catholic merchant who made his fortune in the linen trade and wine excise business. This was, after all, the era of the Dutch East India Company, when the Netherlands became the world's leading maritime and economic force. With his fortune, Hartman bought the house on

Amsterdam's Oudezijds Voorburgwal, along with two attached properties in the adjoining alley. He then set about merging the three attics into one space, to create his own *schuilkerk*, a hidden Catholic house church.

Despite the prohibition of religious observance, Our Dear Lord in the Attic was a well-known 'secret'. The Protestant authorities were happy to turn a blind eye. As long as the church was unidentifiable from the outside, they would tolerate what went on within – a liberal attitude that endures in the city to this day. With space for 150 worshippers, who packed into the neat nave and up into the two levels of galleries, the church served a whole community for over 200 years. From its completion in 1663 until the dedication of the far larger Saint Nicolas's Church in 1887, this divine loft conversion hosted weddings, baptisms and masses; Hartman, given his connections in the trade, was able to provide the communion wine.

Ons' Lieve Heer op Solder still springs a surprise. Tucked into De Wallen – Amsterdam's Red Light District – it's a sliver of saintliness amid sin. There are sex shops and brothels just around the corner yet, within this house – now a museum – 17th-century bourgeois decorum remains. The lower floors look just as Hartman might have left them, from the Delft-tiled kitchens to the grandstanding *zaal* (main parlour), with its marble-flanked fireplace, fine furniture and ceiling of gilded oak.

Above, on the second floor, is a simple confessional, installed around 1740 so the priest might better forgive the confider's sins. On the third floor, up the time-worn stairs, lies the big reveal: the church, preserved here in its 19th-century glory. Just as in 1862, rush matting covers the floors while electric replicas of the old gaslights hang from the roof and walls. The woodwork is painted *caput mortuum* ('dead head'), a liverish shade of pink, which seems to channel the eye to the fine altarpiece, where Christ's baptism sits below the stucco of God the Father and the Holy Spirit, depicted as a dove.

Outside, Amsterdam rumbles, the canal busy with boats, the restaurants, bars and brothels doing a roaring trade. But up here, in this God-fearing garret, there's a hidden place of peace, where you might feel closer to the divine, no matter what your beliefs.

| | |
|---|---|
| Where? | Languedoc-Roussillon, France |
| What? | Isolated hilltop stronghold where the last of the Cathars hid out |

## MONTSÉGUR

THE SCENE is dramatic rather than barbaric. Looking out from the ruins marooned atop this precipitous bluff, the Pyrenean foothills weave and fade into the heat haze. Trees cling to the steep limestone slopes and the sweet optimism of wildflowers perfumes the breeze. Somewhere down below, a little village is tucked into the lee of the valley, where a bakery sells crusty bread and a terrace café serves excellent Vin de Pays d'Oc. And yet, such horrors happened here. This tumbled castle – so formidable, so seemingly out of reach – was once the final hideout of a religious group ruthlessly persecuted for their beliefs. Within these thick ramparts, upon this lofty peak, several hundred of these hounded souls sought refuge, making their last stand against extinction ...

The French region of Languedoc-Roussillon, sprawling sublime and sun-kissed around the shores of the Mediterranean up to the heights of the Pyrenees, feels classic France: olive groves and vineyards, river gorges, forests and pretty little towns of cobbles and cafés. However, it was far from idyllic for the Cathars, a Christian sect that developed between the 11th and 14th centuries and once dared to dispute the theology of Rome.

Cathars were scattered all over Europe, but thrived particularly in the historically tolerant frontier region of southwest France. Zealous and devoted, they believed in two gods – one good, one bad; a tenet in direct opposition to the monotheistic Catholic church. Also, they thought the body was nothing but a prison for the genderless human spirit; a vessel to keep it trapped in the evil, material realm until death released it unto heaven. The Cathars,

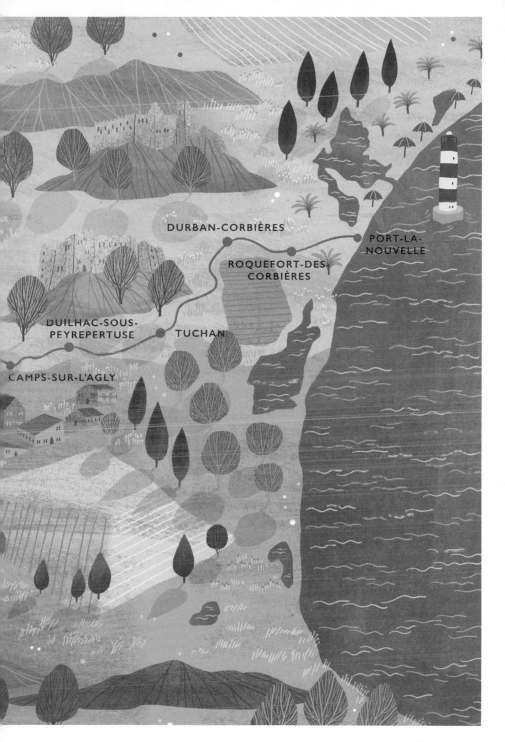

DURBAN-CORBIÈRES

ROQUEFORT-DES-CORBIÈRES

PORT-LA-NOUVELLE

DUILHAC-SOUS-PEYREPERTUSE

TUCHAN

CAMPS-SUR-L'AGLY

who lived strictly abstemious lives, thus felt contempt for all material possessions – not least religious relics (which Catholics were encouraged to worship), reproductions of the cross (a symbol of torture) and the lavish robes worn by the Pope himself. Such things, they felt, were not only an irrelevance but a wickedness.

Not surprisingly, this perceived heresy, and the Cathars' rising popularity, angered the Catholic church. So, in 1208, Pope Innocent III announced a crusade to eliminate them. Over the following 40 years, battles were fought, sieges were staged and massacres were perpetrated. The Cathars were forced to fight, to convert or to hide, with some choosing to retreat to a handful of remote castles in the foothills of the Pyrenees.

Today, tourism brains have dubbed this history-saturated region of fortified hills, towns and villages le Pays Cathare (Cathar Country). Also, a long-distance hiking trail, the Sentier Cathare (Cathar Way), runs for over a hundred miles, linking the strongholds where the 'heretics' held out. Or at least versions of them. After the crusade, many of the so-called Cathar castles were rebuilt, often on the same sites, to defend France's new southern border. In some places – such as Béziers, Beaucaire and Muret – nothing much remains. However, while the masonry may be lost, the stories remain, vividly conjuring Languedoc's bloody past.

That's nowhere more true than at Montségur, a forbidding ruin sitting 1,200 metres (3,940 feet) up, atop a pog (volcanic pluton). In the local Occitan language, Montségur means 'safe hill', and for a while it was just that. The castle here became a refuge for *faidits* – dispossessed Cathars seeking a safe space. In 1233 Montségur became the seat of the Cathar church. It also became a key target.

Looking at it today, it still seems impressively impenetrable, perched so high and stout, sheer cliff faces on one side. However, penetrated it was. In May 1243, around 10,000 troops lay siege to Montségur, inside which around 500 people cowered. Against overwhelming odds, the Cathars held out for months. But finally the Crusaders managed a successful attack and surrender became inevitable. At the end of a short truce, those willing to adopt the Catholic faith were permitted to walk away. Those that would not faced a grizzlier fate. On 16 March 1244, some 225 unrepentant Cathars processed out of Montségur and descended to a field where a bonfire blazed. There were too many of them to tie to individual stakes, so they were herded into an enclosure and burned alive in the flames.

Now, the village of Montségur is reached via a switchbacking road amid the foothills. From the village it's a short, steep hike up to the castle looming above, the trail passing right through the Prat dels Cremats (Field of the Burned). Here, a stele commemorates the slaughter; its Occitan inscription dedicates it to 'the Cathars, martyrs of pure Christian love'. Flowers are often placed here. Beyond the field, the path continues up – no doubt one of the network of paths used by sympathetic villagers who managed to sneak supplies behind the besieged walls. From the top the views are spectacular, stretching over limestone crags and ripples of cow-grazed green. On a clear day the castles of Puivert and Roquefixade might just be spied in the distance.

The Cathar fortress of Montségur was demolished after its capture in 1244. The current fortress, with its square keep and walled courtyard, is the result of three centuries of subsequent rebuilding and renovation, plus many more of neglect. However, a few traces of original Cathar buildings can be seen just north of the present walls. And simply standing within the stark, empty stone shell, in this isolated and heaven-reaching location, seems to echo both the Cathar's austerity and their spiritual aspiration.

Where? Tirol, Austria

What?     Idyllic Alpine valley, only
          reachable on foot

KAISERTAL

KAISERTAL, POPULATION: 39. A valley
largely disconnected from the modern
world, yet completely connected to Mother
Nature. This geological slice through the
Alps roars not with automobiles but with
rivers, ice-clear torrents that rush down the great grey gorge, amid
the fir forest and wildflowers, around cliff crags and pastures of
lush, flower-flecked green, beneath the soaring, snowy tops of the
Kaiser (Emperor) Mountains. This is a place out of time, where
ingress is on foot, the rhythm is slow, wildlife is protected and man
has made only the most minimal mark ...

The Kaisertal valley, tucked between the Tirolean towns of
Kufstein and Ebbs, near the German border, isn't easy to reach.
It was the last inhabited valley in Austria to be reached by road. For
as long as anyone can remember, essentials such as food and fuel
were hauled up via a rickety aerial ropeway. The few vehicles used
for navigating within the Kaisertal itself had to be winched up or
flown in; thus stranded, they were driven without licence plates or
the eye of the law, earning the Kaisertal the moniker 'Valley of the
Outlaws'. In 2008, with the boring of the 820-metre (2,690-foot)
Kaisertal Tunnel, tarmac finally linked this isolated Alpine settlement
to the rest of the country – but only for a select few: residents,
service providers and emergency services have a card that can
open the gates. For everyone else, the tunnel is off-limits. As it
always has been, the only way for curious visitors to enter the
Kaisertal is to leave their cars behind and walk.

Clearly, humans have settled here for millennia. As well as the
remains of cave bears, lion and hyena, archaeological excavations at

the valley's deep Tischofer Cave have unearthed bone tools made by paleo-human people, dated to around 28,000 years ago – the oldest evidence of human presence yet found in the Tirol. The cave also appears to have been used as a workshop during the Stone Age. More recently it was a hideout and weapons cache for Tirolean rebels during the Napoleonic Wars; the freedom fighters placed a desk inside, so referred to visiting the cave as going *'tisch oba'* (up to the desk), spawning its current name. Witches are said to lurk hereabouts too, a theory all too believable when you venture through the cave's gaping entrance and walk deep, deep, deeper into the blackness, the damp and the cool caressing your skin like a spirit's touch.

From Ebbs, it's a climb of around 285 steps on the Kaiseraufstieg path into the Kaisertal, a testing but worth-it ascendance into a perfect Alpine playground. The Kaisertal lies within the Kaisergebirge Nature Reserve, encapsulating the Wilder (Wild) and Zahmer (Tame) Kaiser Mountains. Here, chamois pose upon the outcrops and red deer bellow from the slopes. Look skyward for the outspread wings of gliding golden eagles; glance down to spy yellow lady's slipper orchids, blue gentians, rare dwarf *Alpenrosen* and abundant mountain cowslip. This is an apple strudel idyll of meadows and mountain majesty, of gentle farmsteads, lung-clearing forests and steep rock walls rising to fearsome peaks. Of thunking cowbells and buzzing bees. Of mile upon mile of hiking trails and *gemütliche* huts serving fresh cheese, home-baked *Kuchen*, cold beer and bonhomie. Of geranium-draped balconies and the simple, whitewashed walls of the 18th-century Antoniuskapelle, its neat steeple rising in praise of the mighty mountains behind.

People do still live in the Kaisertal, albeit in dwindling numbers. The Hinterkaiser, the oldest farm in the valley, has a deed of sale dating back to the Middle Ages. While the lure of convenience is great for some, so is the simplicity of staying put. For some there's no bigger joy than living a little off-grid, in tune with the seasons, at a dialled-down pace, in a place of peace, where the crowds will never come.

| | |
|---|---|
| Where? | Baden-Württemberg, Germany |
| What? | Deep, dark woodland haunted by myth and magic |

## BLACK FOREST

WHAT WAS that? Something sneaking through the trees? Though it's hard to see under this heavy canopy of green. Any further than an arm's length and the world is lost to bark and bough; an arboreal army, obstructing anything beyond – if indeed there *is* a beyond. The thick, unfathomable forest seems like its own planet, an enclosed system governed by different rules. A dominion where fairies might dance amid the mushrooms, men might turn into wolves, sorcerers might fire bullets that can bend around trees. Everything is hidden and mysterious in this realm where all things – magical and macabre – might happen ...

Physically, the Black Forest (the Schwarzwald) cloaks southwest Germany, from Karlsruhe to the Upper Danube and from Pforzheim to Lörrach. Psychologically, it seeps much further. This expanse of oak, elm, beech and pine, pasture, streams and mountains, castles, monasteries, moss and mist has become the stuff of legend; the backdrop for stories and nightmares for people around the globe.

Roman soldiers called it Silva Nigra (Black Wood) on account of its darkness and utter impenetrability. Dense, pitch, roamed by who knows what, it was a menacing, terrifying place. In a forest this thick, you could be lost in a few ill-made footsteps or easily spooked by strange noises or flickering shadows. It's a quirk of the forest: as vision becomes restricted by so many trees, so the imagination runs far and wild.

No surprise then that this German jungle is so rich in folklore and fairy tale. There are stories of werewolves, witches and wizards; of headless horsemen that ride fine white steeds; of a lake haunted

by an undead king who grabs women to take to his underwater lair. The Grimm Brothers found inspiration here while compiling their book of traditional stories in the early 19th century. For instance, it's believed Hansel and Gretel became hopelessly lost amid these trees. More than simple entertainment, such fables – not originally intended for children – often had political and social undertones. During the 14th century, when the Great Famine gripped Europe, it seems quite reasonable that a pair of children might be hungry enough to eat a house.

One such place of Black Forest legend is the Feldsee, a secretive, circular lake laying in the lee of the Feldberg, Germany's highest mountain outside of the Alps. Sitting over 1,100 metres (3,600 feet) above sea level, hemmed in by steep slopes on three sides, the glacial lake is only reachable on foot or by bike. As such, it remains peaceful – maybe even enchanted ...

So the story goes, at nearby Saint Blaise Abbey lived two monks who were uncommonly cruel and delighted in tormenting their younger brothers. Not content with a lifetime of sadism, when they died they continued to haunt the place, bedevilling the monks from beyond the grave. Word of this wickedness reached a devout Capuchin friar in the town of Staufen who, possessed of ancient knowledge, came to the abbey and exorcised the evil spirits, ensnaring them in a sack, which he threw from the top of the Feldberg. The sack and its callous cargo tumbled down into the Feldsee – and there the ghouls might have remained, to harrow any passing souls. However, they were seen off by the *Erdmännlein* – 'earth men' or dwarves, who are known for their kindness.

The Feldsee lies within the Southern Black Forest Nature Park, where yellow gentian and silver thistle grow, deer graze, squirrels scamper and the forest – which, over the centuries, has been altered and reduced – is being managed to maintain some of its legendary wildness. A trail leads right around the lakeshore, so you can view it from every aspect. But it's forbidden to swim in the Feldsee's waters. They say it's because of the spiny quillwort, a rare underwater fern, which thrives in the shallows. Or perhaps it's to protect bathers from the phantoms of the past.

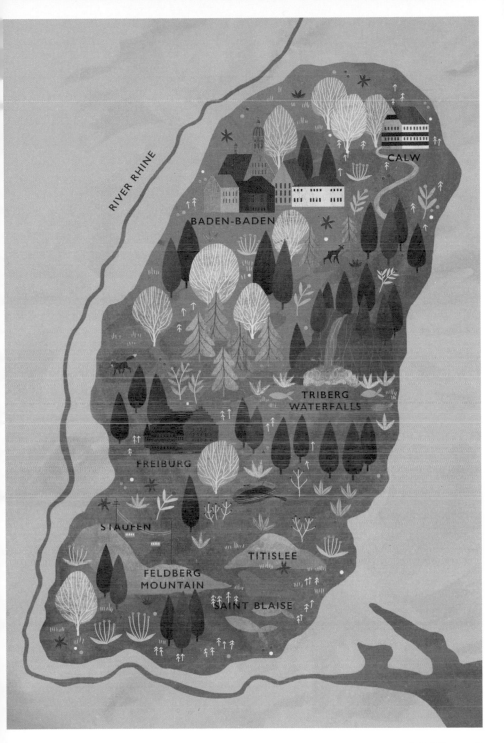

RIVER RHINE

CALW

BADEN-BADEN

TRIBERG
WATERFALLS

FREIBURG

STAUFEN

TITISLEE

FELDBERG
MOUNTAIN

SAINT BLAISE

## RÖK RUNESTONE

HIDDEN IN plain sight for centuries, the stone kept its secret. While prayers to the new faith slid over its surface, while the old ways of which it spoke were usurped by Father, Son and Holy Spirit, it sat – stoically, solidly, strong as a Viking. Biding its time. A hefty slab of pale-grey, fine-grained granite, no one guessed its significance. While the slab helped support a modest house of God, it also silently held a story of a different world and time, just waiting to be reread ...

The Rök runestone (a menhir inscribed with runic script) is one of Sweden's most fascinating finds. The country's finest known runestone, it's thought to have been carved around AD 800, in the late Viking age, with considerable skill and dexterity. But for nearly 1,000 years, it was completely forgotten – despite being there for all to see.

Somewhere between the Rök runestone's creation and the establishment of Christianity in Sweden, in around the mid-12th century, its original purpose was either accidentally overlooked or wilfully obscured. As the old Norse belief system lost favour to the words of the Bible, the runestone was unceremoniously recycled into the walls of a Christian church – common practice for these then-redundant mementoes of a pagan age. No longer revered; reduced to masonry.

The Rök stone sat, unknown and unloved, until 1843, when builders discovered that it didn't only have writing on its visible side, but on five sides. They made a note, but still the stone was left in place. It was only in 1862 that it was removed from its

Christian confines and installed in the churchyard outside, where it remains today.

Thus revealed, its message becomes clear – that is, if you can read and interpret runic, the ancient alphabet used to write Germanic languages before Latin became the letter system of choice. Rising 2.5 metres (8 feet) from the ground (with a sizeable chunk buried beneath), the granite monolith is inscribed with 760 characters, which flow all around its flanks. Runestones, of which there are up to 2,500 in Sweden – far more than in any other country – were primarily monuments to the deceased, usually to powerful people, recording their noble deeds; the Rök stone was thought to speak of a Viking called Varin, weaving a tale of gods, grief, valour and victories, of an era long past. It was clearly an object of some importance: the name of the stone has been traced back to the people who first rediscovered it in the 19th century; they named it after the nearby village of Rök, in the quiet lakelands of central Sweden. But the village itself was most likely named after the stone in the first place (Rök meaning 'skittle-shaped stack or stone') long before it ended up in the church wall.

Although this menhir has finally been revealed, its message remains hidden. The runes are largely written in a Swedish–Norwegian 16-character alphabet. But there are also lines in Futhark, an older runic script. And, to further complicate matters, a cipher was used to encrypt the engravings. Despite the fact the runes are clear and easy to read, the length of the inscription and its enigmatic execution have rendered it impossible to wholly understand.

Many translations suggest that the stone was erected by Varin to honour his dead son, and perhaps to fortify his own status by declaring his formidable lineage. It was believed to detail wars and warriors; the battlefield described in the text has been linked to the legendary Battle of Brávellir, said to have taken place not far from Rök in the mid-eighth century. Norse god Thor, the valkyrie Gunnr and sixth-century Ostrogothic king Theodoric the Great all make an appearance too. But later theories suggest the message may not be about heroic deeds at all, but rather about the power of writing itself, in its ability to memorialise the dead, to last the ages. Even if it gets lost for a few hundred years.

| What? | Forgotten summer house of a Roman emperor, spilling into the bright blue sea |

## VILLA OF TIBERIUS

TO GAZE out from this grotto, to the sun-sparkled Mediterranean, is to look with the eyes of legends. From the cool, water-dripped shadows, you behold the same view seen by Odysseus, King of Ithaca, who paused here on his way back home from Troy; you peer out like Emperor Tiberius, who feasted and frolicked in this coastal hidey-hole, to escape from the Senate and Rome. Yet, for millennia, this cavern remained concealed. The town around, itself named after caves just like it, kept this particular subterranean treasure a hidden secret ...

Emperor Tiberius, adopted son and successor of Augustus Caesar, the first Roman emperor, ruled from AD 14 to AD 37. By all accounts he wasn't handsome, popular or particularly pleasant – Pliny the Elder called him *tristissimus hominum* (the gloomiest of men). Nor, it seems, did he much relish his role. As his reign progressed, Tiberius distanced himself from the capital, preferring to spend his time in southern Italy, shirking responsibility for life as a morally questionable recluse. He built several villas, including a dozen on the island of Capri; the ruins of three still remain. But it was also known that Tiberius had a summer residence on the mainland, somewhere between Naples and Rome, along the ancient coast road; contemporaneous historians wrote of his 'villa called the Grotto', allegedly near the town of Terracina. But no one knew exactly where.

Fast forward to 1957, and the builders of a new seaside highway made an incredible discovery. Mere metres from the old town of Sperlonga, at the base of Monte Ciannito, they found an

archaeological bounty: the remains of rooms, a courtyard, pools, ponds and grandiose statuary fit for a king.

Sperlonga is a picturesque jumble of alleys, roof terraces and whitewashed houses draped with bougainvillea that spills down to two magnificent golden beaches. Its original name, Spelunca, derives from the Latin *speluncae*, meaning 'sea caves', many of which are gnawed into the golden Tyrrhenian coast. Evidence of human habitation, dating back to the Upper Palaeolithic era, has been found here. Evidence that Sperlonga is the site of Amyclae, the mythical Spartan city that mysteriously disappeared some 3,000 years ago, is thinner on the ground, though that hasn't stopped the claims.

The Sperlonga villa had been in Tiberius's family for several generations. It was reportedly a sumptuous multi-storey residence, spreading up the hillside and incorporating a natural sea cave that was converted into an opulent banqueting hall, decorated with marble panels, *mascheroni* (grotesque masks) and imposing statues. Here, Tiberius and his guests would loll on rock-hewn beds and dine on an artificial island set within an ornamental, fish-filled pool; it's said that food was floated across on miniature boats.

After the collapse of the Western Roman Empire in the sixth century, locals used the then-ruined villa as a refuge from Saracen attacks. The entire town was razed in 1534 by the pirate Barbarossa, while nature took its course, burying Tiberius's bolthole beneath mounds of sand. Sperlonga's fortunes changed briefly in the mid-20th century. Just as its precious remains were unearthed, so the town was being discovered by the glamorous jet set, with actors such as Brigitte Bardot drawn to this sunny and spectacular easy escape from Rome.

Sperlonga is no longer so in vogue, but the villa remains captivating. The site lies at the end of a long, lovely beach, marked by a cavern so gaping it seems impossible it was ever lost. Adjacent to the site, a museum now displays the treasures found inside the grotto, including huge reconstructed sculptures representing stories from the *Odyssey*: the assault of Scylla, Odysseus lifting Achilles's corpse, the blinding of the cyclops Polyphemus. Little decoration remains within the grotto itself. Here, you're free to roam, following the low stone walls, walking around the ponds and entering the cave itself – a natural nick in the limestone that once held some of the most powerful men in the world.

Where?   Asturias, Spain

What?    Ancient mountain village,
         still only accessible by
         funicular or foot

**BULNES**

IN THIS tiny cliff-squeezed village, life is – and always has been – lived vertically. 'Flat' is scarce a thing in lofty Bulnes. All is up or down. Tough or tougher. No planes land here; no cars swing by. For centuries the sole way in was to walk the well-worn tracks, no wider than a mule; a slow, relentless, zig-zagging haul from the valley bottom, amid tumbled rock, holm oaks, bears and wolves. Now the modern world is knocking at the door of this lonely hamlet in the hills, but it still feels like Mother Nature is in charge ...

The Picos de Europa got their name, so they say, because this hulking mass of mountains, close to northern Spain's Cantabrian coast, was the first glimpse of Europe for sailors returning from the Americas. After adventuring in the New World and spending weeks at sea, it must have been quite a homecoming to see all this looming limestone – topping out at over 2,500 metres (8,200 feet) – suddenly hove into view.

And somewhere amid that massif is Bulnes, a remote little village of no more than 50 people, hiding 650 metres (2,130 feet) up a side valley off the mighty Cares Gorge. That humans thought to settle there seems incredible; that they have remained there for millennia even more so.

The Picos de Europa, designated a national park in 1918, have been inhabited since Palaeolithic times, though it wasn't until around 2,500 years ago that people here began the practice of transhumance – moving livestock with the seasons. This agricultural method has shaped both the landscape and culture of these seemingly inhospitable mountains. It's evolved a hardy breed of

men and women who know how to survive in this terrain. It's created a unique local cuisine, in which you can taste the very pastures on which the animals graze. And it's spawned a web of villages among the nooks and crannies that are, by necessity, close enough to be walked between.

It's also engendered a legendary indomitability. Maze-like, gorge-riven and swathed in impenetrable forests, this portion of Spain has been something of a fortress throughout history; a place where locals could hide from invaders – whoever those invaders might be. When Roman legionnaires came empire-building in the first century BC, the Cantabrian peaks were the last of Iberia to fall. Later, when the Moors were rampant, conquering the Iberian Peninsula, they met their match in the mountains of Asturias. It was here, in AD 722, that heroic Don Pelayo defeated an army of 100,000 Arabs at the Battle of Covadonga, forcing them to divide and retreat, thus kickstarting the long, slow re-Christianisation of Spain.

One phalanx of those retreating Moors – believed to number 63,000 – scarpered away across the central Picos via Bulnes; having made it beyond the hamlet to Sotres (the highest village in the national park), the invaders allegedly got their comeuppance near the village of Cosgaya, where a mighty landslide swept every last one into the Deva River.

Visiting Bulnes today, it seems impossible that such a turning point of history played out, in part, in this sleepy outpost. Life here has moved on a little: in 2001, a funicular railway was burrowed into the limestone, linking Bulnes to the town of Poncebos below. Wagons carrying 28 people at a time depart every half hour; the journey takes just seven minutes. But, for the traveller at least, it's still better to walk. To stride the uphill-all-the-way shepherd trails from Poncebos or Pandébano, marvelling at the mountains.

Bulnes itself is divided in two: lower La Villa and upper Barrio del Castillo. There's not much in either: a church and covered graveyard (to protect it from the snow), farmhouses in varying states of disrepair, a ruined tower (thought to date from the 14th century), a couple of guesthouses and a handful of cafés spooning hearty *fabada* (bean stew). Though low-level tourism has started to penetrate, Bulnes still offers a proper glimpse of traditional Picos life.

| LALIBELA |

HOW PROFOUNDLY imbedded the beliefs are here. Spiritual depth at its most literal; a holy land half hidden underground. The ancient churches of Lalibela don't physically aspire to the heavens; they're at one with the earth. And, though buried, they are very much alive. White-robed pilgrims eddy around the roofs, process along the lichen-crusted walls, enter the sacred recesses, kneel on the rough, rug-covered floors and seek salvation within the stone – as has been done for centuries. Their songs, their drum beats, their prayers, their faith just as they were 1,000 years ago. The same devotion, long sunken into the soil ...

Few places feel as connected to the past as Ethiopia. This is the cradle of humanity, where our ancestors first walked more than three million years ago. Time ticks differently here: not only does the country run to its own Coptic calendar, leaving it around eight years behind the rest of the world, it feels, in places, like the past millennia haven't happened at all.

So it is at Lalibela. This isolated rural outpost – a scatter of thatched *tukul* huts, perched up on the central highlands – would likely be overlooked entirely if it weren't for its buried treasures. And what treasures: 11 medieval churches hand-hewn out of the rock, skilfully carved and still a living, breathing place of worship. While most houses of God reach for the heavens, at Lalibela the devotee must look down – the sunken churches are hardly visibly until you're standing almost on top of them. The architects here chose to burrow rather than build.

BIETE GOLGOTHA MIKAEL

BIETE MASKAL

BIETE MARIAM

BIETE DENAGEL

BIETE GHIORGIS

BIETE MEDHANI ALEM

BIETE AMANUEL

BIETE LEHEM

BIETE QEDDUS MERCOREUS

TE GABRIEL RAPHAEL

BIETE ABBA LIBANOS

The capital of the ancient Zagwe dynasty, the town was originally known as Roha but later renamed for its most celebrated emperor, Gebre Meskel Lalibela. It's said he was destined for greatness from birth, when an auspicious swarm of bees settled on his skin but did not sting; the name Lalibela stems from an archaic Cushitic phrase meaning 'the man bees obey'. Later, aged around seven, he purportedly spent three days receiving divine teachings from the heavens.

Lalibela became emperor in 1181, shortly before the Muslim conquest halted Christian pilgrimages to the Holy Land. According to legend, the emperor had a divine dream about building a 'New Jerusalem', in which an angel gave him the unique building plans: his churches weren't to be raised upwards from wood or stone but excavated from the volcanic rock. Less architecture, more sculpture or work of art.

Labourers, armed only with hammers, iron axes and chisels, bore into the basalt, digging deep trenches to produce freestanding blocks of rock; into these, churches were carved, complete with columns, crosses and archways, storeyed interiors and intricate reliefs. Other chapels were hewn from cliffs and ravines. Tunnels were burrowed between them, drainage canals were created, a waterway was rerouted and renamed the River Jordan.

The accomplishment was extraordinary, though allegedly a team of angels was on hand to help, working the night shift while the men slept. Tales tell of the whole site being completed in 24 years, by the sweat and graft of more than 40,000 people. Actually, it's more likely that Lalibela took shape over several centuries, and that Emperor Lalibela, who ruled until 1221, brought the complex together as one magnificent whole.

Magnificent indeed: Lalibela was among the first 12 World Heritage sites designated by UNESCO in 1978, lauded for its artistic achievement, its influence on Ethiopian Christianity and the historic integrity of both the structures and the landscape in which they rest. But most beguiling of all is their continued life. No dusty ruin, Lalibela is a place of active devotion. Incense still swirls inside the chapels. Smoke still billows, candles still flicker. Pilgrims still come to pray. Chants in ancient Ge'ez, the holy language of the Ethiopian Orthodox Church, still fill the air. Brocade-robed priests still hold aloft golden crosses. Though tourism is beginning to encroach, visiting Lalibela remains a journey in culture and time.

The churches are divided into two main clusters. The group to the northwest of the river includes Biete Medhani Alem (House of the Saviour of the World). Supported by stout, square columns, and measuring 33.5 metres long by 23.5 metres wide by 11.5 metres high (110 feet by 77 feet by 38 feet), it's the largest monolithic church in the world. An arched passageway leads from here to Biete Mariam (House of Mary), where vivid frescoes of biblical scenes and geometric patterns still embellish the ceilings and walls. The southeast group, reached via a network of deep, dark tunnels, contains the oldest churches, cleaved from existing caves. It also contains Biete Amanuel (House of Emmanuel), one of the finest of all. Etched with mighty columns and wood-like cross-beams, it apes the style of the Aksumite Empire, which fell as Zagwe rose.

Lalibela's newest church should be saved for last. Biete Ghiorgis (House of Saint George) is dedicated to Ethiopia's patron saint and sits a little apart from the rest, though it is connected by a narrow passage. They say Saint George actually supervised the church's construction, and was so pleased with the result that he rode his horse over the wall and into the entrance tunnel; the hoof prints can still be seen. It's not the inside that impresses though. Best is to peer over the edge from the top, to look down on this 15-metre (49 foot) high moss-sprouted monolith, carved from the rose-pink tuff, with geometrical precision, into a gigantic Greek-style cross. The symmetry, the scale, the audacity beg only one question: how? And suddenly the input of angels doesn't seem far-fetched at all.

What? Mighty sub-Saharan city
kept under wraps by
colonial powers

## GREAT ZIMBABWE

SUCH PRECISION in stone. A great granite citadel, built without machines or mortar, proudly rising amid the hills of the Zimbabwe plateau, between the Limpopo and Zambezi Rivers. This commanding capital – still striking though in decay – was once home to 20,000 people, a thriving medieval megapolis in the heart of Africa. But over time, the city's truth got lost. No, worse: wilfully hidden. Its story stolen from its rightful forebears to vindicate the new powers in town ...

Great Zimbabwe is the most extensive set of ruins south of the Sahara. Built by the Shona people between the 11th and 15th centuries AD, it was the seat of a powerful kingdom, and a key trading and metal-working hub. Though Portuguese mariners told of an inland 'fortress built of stones of marvellous size' in the mid-16th century, the site was not officially rediscovered by Europeans until 1868. By which time the impressive stonework was a huge inconvenience.

The race for Africa was on, and one justification that the white man could use for colonising the continent was that its people were so obviously inferior, with no history, no sophistication nor ability to develop alone. Thus it must have been some other civilisation – the Egyptians, Arabs or Phoenicians – who created this architectural feat. The presence of exotic items, including Chinese pottery and Arabian glass beads, provided 'evidence' for the idea of external constructors. That those precious items might have found their way to Great Zimbabwe due to its formidable trading status was out of the question. It was simply

unthinkable that black African culture could create something of this style and scale.

The non-African story was perpetuated, despite evidence to the contrary. First to study the site, in 1905, was British-born archaeologist David Randall-MacIver, who concluded it was 'unquestionably African in every detail'. Angry imperialists simply prohibited further excavations. From 1965, the country's ruling white-minority government even ordered the creation of fake news, with fictional origin stories printed in official guidebooks showing that white people were indeed responsible for the site. Great Zimbabwe was there for all to see. But its truth remained hidden.

It was only in 1980, when the troubled colony achieved fully recognised independence, that the story changed. And that these great archaeological remains not only became properly acknowledged but gave their name to this new country: Zimbabwe – the word originates from the Shona *dzimba-hwe* (venerated houses). The ruins were solid proof that Africans had, and could, run their own complex societies. Zimbabwe's cultural history was ready to be rewritten.

The site has three main areas. The Hill Complex, an extensive system of ruins atop a commanding 300-metre (985-foot) mound, is the oldest, and is believed to have been inhabited continuously until the site was abandoned in around 1450, for reasons unknown. It was the spiritual centre, where sacrifices were made; a large bird-shaped boulder is where the king would preside over important matters. The soapstone bird carvings here – which depict birds with human lips and five-fingered feet – now appear on Zimbabwe's flag.

The Valley Complex, a scatter of ruined dry-stone and mud-brick houses, spreads from the base of the hill, but most impressive is the Great Enclosure. This vast, double-walled elliptical compound, dating to the 14th century, is the largest ancient structure in sub-Saharan Africa. Its outer walls, in places as wide as a car and extending 250 metres (820 feet), are constructed from hundreds of thousands of expertly cut granite blocks, stacked without mortar. Between them is a 10-metre (33-foot) high Conical Tower, perhaps a grain store, maybe a symbol of power.

These days monkeys scamper across the fallen rocks and scrub scruffs up the walls. Colonial plundering and ill-managed attempts at reconstruction have taken their toll. But while the structure of Great Zimbabwe has fallen to ruin, at least its history is now intact.

**TURPAN OASIS**

ALL AROUND is desiccated. A sea of gravel. Burnt rock. Parched, puckered slopes rising to a cloudless blue sky. A bone-dry, furnace-hot wind whips, shrivelling the skin, singeing the eyes. So why, in the middle, is there so much green? Despite the climate – scorching summers, freezing winters – the bottom of this barren basin blooms like a promised land, an unlikely eruption of well-watered life. Not the work of Allah, Buddha or Mother Nature, but of man and his ingenious labours under the thirsty soil ...

Flung out in far-western China, where one of the planet's deepest depressions meets the snow-clad Tian Shan Mountains, Turpan is remote, extreme and seemingly inhospitable. It's the hottest city in the country, with record highs pushing 50°C (122°F) – locals call it 'Fire Land'; rain, they say, comes once every ten years. But despite this insalubrious situation, the city has thrived for centuries. An unexpected billow of lushness where such a thing has no right to be.

Turpan is a city of the Silk Road, the fabled ancient trade route linking east and west, spidering across China, India, Central Asia and Persia to reach Constantinople and Rome. Exotic goods – silks, furs, ivory, ideas – were carried thousands of miles. Turpan was a significant stop on a northern branch of the route across China, laying between Hami and the great crossroads city of Kashgar. It must have been a welcome sight for the weary caravans traipsing across these badlands – more than 40 per cent of Xinjiang Province is desert, most of the rest is formidable mountains. In Turpan traders could find inns and markets, maybe a brothel or two.

But fewer travellers would have stopped here were it not for the *karez* – meaning 'well' in the language of the Uyghur, the local Turkic Muslim peoples. Turpan's *karez* systems, comprising ingenious underground labyrinths of channels, are the arteries of the city, the reason it can survive. They harvest the clear meltwater from the mighty Tian Shan and divert it to the Turpan basin, turning a riverless dust bowl into a bountiful oasis.

Karez technology was invented by the Persians in the seventh century BC and slowly spread. Historians are unsure when the know-how arrived in Turpan – some say around 100 BC, others think much later – but at some point, Silk Road traders travelling east from modern-day Iraq and Iran came bearing engineering nous; the methodology was then developed by the Uyghurs. Turpan is the only place in China where such a system can be seen.

Though 'seen' is a misnomer. The majority of this architectural feat is hidden beneath the earth, to protect it from contamination and the fierce, evaporative sun. The whole network is immense, including over 1,000 – possibly up to 1,700 – *karez* systems, each comprising vertical wells, subterranean troughs, tree-shaded surface canals and little reservoirs. While most *karez* are around 3 kilometres (1.9 miles) long, some are ten times that, with hundreds of wells dug at regular intervals to provide access and ventilation; in total, there could be up to 5,000 kilometres (3,100 miles) of channels burrowed underground.

Today, many of the *karez* have run dry, due to industrialisation and climate change. It's estimated that only 200 or so are still functioning. But while the ancient engineering may be in decline, you can still see its results. This man-made water supply has helped Turpan become a hub of grape-growing. Vine-weaved trellises, heavy with a dozen types of grapes, shade every garden, and the landscape is scattered with *chunches*, aerated mud-brick towers where bunches are hung to dry into famously sweet raisins. Apricots, mulberries and melons also rely on the *karez* – as do the people. When the mercury soars, and the hot wind scalds, the inhabitants of Turpan take their lives underground, sitting in the natural cool, chatting over fresh-plucked grapes, hiding from the harshness, just as their ancestors did long ago.

| Where? | Siem Reap Province, Cambodia |
| --- | --- |
| What? | Long-concealed birthplace of the Khmer Empire |

## PHNOM KULEN

SOMEWHERE, BENEATH the rare ancient hardwoods and the cashew nut plantations, the tangled vines and trip-you-up roots, the rubber plants and the banana bushes, the red biting ants and trilling cicadas, an entire city rests. And not just any city. The city that was the origin of a mighty empire, the most powerful the region has ever known, in charge for more than 600 years. It housed god-like kings, cleverly re-engineered the wilderness and provided inspiration for the world's greatest religious complex. For centuries the once-great capital has slept, lying fitfully beneath a heavy blanket of verdure and neglect; crumbled, decrepit, crippled by nature, war and time. But now, thanks to new technology, its glories are starting to re-emerge ...

The Khmer Empire began in modern-day Cambodia and, at its peak, ruled most of mainland Southeast Asia. Specifically it began at Phnom Kulen – the Mountain of the Lychee – a long, serpent-like sandstone plateau that rises as high as 500 metres (1,640 feet) above the flat Angkorian plain. It was here, in AD 802, that King Jayavarman II declared independence from the kingdoms of Java and, in a ritual performed by a Brahmin priest, was pronounced *chakravartin* (universal monarch or king of the world).

At that time Phnom Kulen was known as Mahendraparvata, the Mountain of Indra, King of the Gods. It was resource rich, with plentiful sandstone that could be quarried for building and a reliable water supply: a spring on the holy mountain is the source of the Siem Reap River, which flows south past Angkor into the Tonlé Sap Lake. Bamboo rafts loaded with stone

could float away down this channel to facilitate the building of temples elsewhere.

Mahendraparvata was a masterstroke of town planning. Arranged around a mountain-topping royal palace, temples and houses lined wide boulevards and a complex network of dykes, dams, ponds and canals was built to control and divert water across the plateau. The ninth-century city also contributed to the wonder of Angkor, around 30 kilometres (19 miles) further south. The eventual capital of the Khmer Empire – not to mention one of the world's most impressive sites – Angkor represents the peak of Khmer ingenuity, craftsmanship and style. But the sophistication of Phnom Kulen's Hindu temples and expert hydraulics served as a template. Even after its tenure as capital ended, Kulen remained occupied, right up until the empire fell in the 15th century. Then – just like Angkor – it was largely abandoned.

Phnom Kulen was officially 'rediscovered' in 2012. Archaeologists had long surmised that Mahendraparvata might lie buried on this particular mountain, and an aerial survey, using hi-tech laser technology, provided confirmation – and showed it to be far more extensive than previously believed. But while the notion of a 'lost city re-found' is romantic, it's not quite true. Cambodians and their ancestors have been living in this area for thousands of years; a handful of villages remain scattered across Phnom Kulen, where subsistence farmers tend their beans and rice paddies, living in stilted wooden huts. Even if most of the world weren't aware, they have never forgotten the significance of this sacred summit.

Exploring Phnom Kulen today takes determination. Most travellers have neither time nor inclination to leave the majestic ruins of Angkor in order to spend a few days bouncing over clay-sticky, pot-holed backroads, clambering and bushwhacking through grow-back-as-quick-as-you-scythe-it jungle, getting thorn-snagged and bug-bitten to see far less immediately impressive ruins. Most who do venture this way get only as far as the River of A Thousand Lingas, where the phallic symbols of Shiva have been carved into a riverbed, and to the temple of Preah Ang Thom, where a gilded Buddha reclines and pilgrims flock in droves.

But it's worth probing further, to get beyond the crowds and to the heart of this ancient empire. To do so requires local knowledge; someone who knows not only where the ruins are and how to navigate the paths between them, but someone who knows where it's safe to roam. Thanks to its strategic yet hard-to-reach location, Phnom Kulen served as a stronghold for the brutal Khmer Rouge from 1970 until the mid-1990s. From here, these fanatical Communist fighters could hide out and perform acts of sabotage. As a result of their presence, the mountain was both bombed and laid with mines – B-52 craters dint the ground, and unexploded ordnance and landmines remain a serious hazard.

But with a good guide, the mountain will reveal some of its secrets; its vine-strung towers and temples, its ancient brickwork besmirched by lichen and overgrown with bushes and lotus flowers. For instance, navigate the scrub to find the temple of O'Thma Dap, where reliefs of leaves and garlands can still be seen on the age-worn stucco, and Prasat O'Paong, a towering, tangerine-coloured triumph, still standing proud amid the jungle. At Sras Damrei (Elephant Pond), an enormous, moss-fuzzed elephant – hewn from a single sandstone block – stands guarded by lions. At Poeng Tbal, you can admire Shiva, Vishnu and a row of wise men carved into the rock.

Most significant, though, is Rong Chen, a multi-tiered pyramid of sandstone and rust-red laterite that sits at the plateau's highest point. It was the centrepiece of the royal city, and the very spot where Jayavarman II was made god like king, kickstarting the superpower that would shape the region for centuries, only to lie largely hidden for many more.

| Where? | Ryukyu Islands, Japan |
|---|---|
| What? | A mysterious underwater monument, of origins unknown |

## YONAGUNI

WHAT MYSTERY is this, sunken in the blue? Amid the warm wave-chop, where Pacific Ocean meets South China Sea, a large and incongruous mass of rock sits fully submerged in the realm of the fishes. And yet it looks curiously man-made. Columns rise, flat walls soar, gaps seem cut through like corridors, blocks squat like buildings, neat steps are carved at sharp angles – a little too perfect to be natural. Is it simply a freak of submarine geology? Or could it be the remnants of an ancient civilisation long lost beneath the waves …

At the very extreme of the Ryukyu archipelago, the island chain that dangles into the subtropics from the major Japanese isle of Kyushu, sits little Yonaguni. The island marks Japan's southwesternmost tip, just 110 kilometres (68 miles) from the coast of Taiwan. And, though it was once an important trading centre, there's little there now: a handful of villages, a wind-whipped lighthouse, a few cows and wild horses. But the turquoise waters that lap this outpost harbour far greater intrigue. Indeed, most visitors who make the effort to visit Yonaguni come for the diving: a resplendence of colourful corals, bright fish, huge gatherings of hammerhead sharks – and a sub-aqua enigma.

Yonaguni-jima Kaitei Iseki (the Yonaguni Island Submarine Ruins) were discovered on the southern side of the island, off Iseki Point, by local diver Kihachiro Aratake in the mid-1980s. He was scouring for good hammerhead sites when he came across the 'ruins': a rectangular formation measuring about 27 metres (90 feet) tall, its apex just 5 metres (16 feet) below sea level. The structure, which is also known as the Iseki stones, comprises a range of features,

including a pair of pillars, a triangular depression, a star-shaped platform and semi-regular terraces that some have likened to Maya pyramids. The rock itself – a mix of sandstone and mudstone – is thought to date back around 20 million years. But some believe its shaping was done by human hands, around 10,000 years ago. If so, that means Yonaguni predates the Egyptian pyramids.

According to some experts, the strangely unnatural-looking angles and formations of Yonaguni are simply normal examples of sandstone stratigraphy – Geology 101. Sandstone tends to crack along straight planes, especially in areas with high levels of tectonic activity. Yonaguni sits along the Pacific Rim of Fire, along which 90 per cent of the world's earthquakes occur. This scientific explanation hasn't stopped the speculation, however, and wilder theories abound: Yonaguni might be the work of aliens, some say, or even proof of the legendary lost continent of Mu, the Pacific Ocean's Atlantis.

Certainly there are those who remain convinced that this underwater wonder was hewn by man, most likely during the last ice age, when the land was above water and Yonaguni formed part of a land bridge that linked the island to Taiwan. As evidence for this, believers point to the strategically placed round holes, the precisely positioned columns and the etchings that are said to resemble Kaida, the pictograms once used across Japan's southwestern islands. Marine geologist Masaaki Kimura has spent almost 20 years diving and studying Yonaguni; he claims to be able to identify a castle, a pyramid, roads and even a stadium within the formation. Japan's Agency for Cultural Affairs disagrees, refusing to designate Yonaguni as a historical cultural site.

No matter whatever or whoever formed this conundrum of the seas, the island is still a hotspot for divers. All around Yonaguni there are spectacular sites: cliff-like walls, swim-throughs and caves; water brimming with jacks and snapper, turtles and trevally, marlin and cuttlefish, vibrant soft corals and swaying fans. Then there's the chance to explore the ruins themselves. Divers enter via a small tunnel that opens onto a large flat area – much like a ceremonial square – where two columns stand, side by side. Swimming up and down passages, over the neatly perpendicular terraces, even the greatest sceptic might start to wonder if perhaps Yonaguni might have been a manmade wonder after all ...?

| | |
|---|---|
| Where? | Northern Territory, Australia |
| What? | Repository of remote rock art, that only a few are permitted to see |

## MOUNT BORRADAILE

THE LAND across the East Alligator River isn't like the rest of Australia. The air is heavy with the buzz of flies, the punch of the sun and 50,000 years of human history that feels as immediate as yesterday. This is a landscape of another time, an ancient sandstone massif that has tilted over the eons to form a scalded escarpment cut through with caves and fissures. It's a landscape of blood-red dirt and lime-green forest; of jacana – 'Jesus birds' – walking on the billabongs and prehistoric-looking crocs eyeballing from the rivers. It's a place of both bounty and danger, full of sustenance – but only for those who know the ways to find it. And drawn onto this aged canvas is a unique montage that tells the lost stories of the world's oldest civilisation ...

Arnhem Land is one of the planet's least inhabited regions. A remote reserve, bigger than Scotland, lying at the northernmost reaches of the Northern Territory, it is home to no more than 16,000 people. And it is one of the last redoubts of Indigenous Australian culture.

The name is of colonial origin. In 1623 Dutch explorer Willem van Colster sailed along Australia's northeast coast in his ship, *Arnhem*; when the area was declared an Aboriginal Reserve in 1931, the name 'Arnhem Land' stuck. But that doesn't alter its nature. The area is – unlike anywhere else in the country – almost entirely the domain of the Aboriginal people, many of whom reside in small outstations, far from the influence of Western culture, seeking to live in their traditional ways. It's another Australia within Australia. No *balanda* (white people) are allowed in without a

permit; even then, areas of especially deep cultural significance remain off-limits. There is little in the way of modern development – huge tracts of Arnhem Land look just as you imagine they might have done for the past several millennia.

Indeed, it's believed Aboriginal clan groups have occupied this north-coast outpost for 57,000 years. For a hunter-gatherer society, it must have been ideal. There are slow-moving rivers and billabongs replete with fish. There are forests full of birds and edible and medicinal plants. There is bush a-bounce with kangaroos. And there are rocks, ravines and cliffs to provide shelter from the merciless Top End weather – as well as an extensive natural gallery space.

Australia has around 100,000 recorded rock art sites of outstanding age, spirituality and sophistication. These are not merely pretty pictures daubed on stone; these sites offer a priceless glimpse into the past. While there is no written record of the travails of Aboriginal society, their story is part told in these pictograms. They are snapshots of their experience, describing everything from the now-extinct animals they once hunted to their first contact with the wider world. Yet this colourful, incredible historical repository remains relatively unvisited. The story of the world's oldest civilisation curiously under-read.

The whole of Arnhem Land is flush with rock art. But maybe best is Mount Borradaile – or Awunbarna as it's known to the Amurdak people, the area's traditional custodians. Amid the maze of weathered cliffs and gullies, resplendent art in vivid reds, yellows and white seems to grace every wall. Some rocks are an exuberantly jumbled palimpsest, with newer images scrawled on top of older ones, sketches layered like geological strata. How old the oldest are isn't precisely known. The paint was made from powdered rock, containing no organic matter that can be carbon-dated. But there are some clues: a drawing of a thylacine (Tasmanian tiger), which has been extinct here for thousands of years; the presence of a painting beneath an ancient wasps' nest, itself proven to be 20,000 years old.

Aboriginal culture did not fare well on the arrival of white settlers, and was further decimated in the 20th century, when government edicts ordered Aboriginal people off their ancestral lands and forcibly took children away from their families. As a result, so much Aboriginal culture was lost, and that which remains is often kept closely guarded by an unsurprisingly untrusting indigenous population. The Amurdak still own and manage the Mount Borradaile area but, in the 1980s, decided to open it up via an exclusive ecotourism venture. Since then, although some sacred locations remain out of bounds, more of its secrets have been revealed to outsiders, and new sites have been rediscovered.

This wilderness is a gargantuan gallery, etched with eons of characters and legends. There's an abundance of animals, from snakes and dugongs to long-neck turtles, wallabies and even Tasmanian devils, long vanished from this part of Australia. There are Aboriginal spirits, including a huge Rainbow Serpent – a creator-god of Aboriginal mythology – writhing across an overhang, tongue licking through its tombstone teeth. There are bodies everywhere: waving hands, twisted stick figures, alien-like faces, internal organs, sexual anatomy. Many later works – called 'contact art', often drawn over pre-existing works – tell a different story, depicting the ships, rifles, pipe-smoking buffalo hunters and men on horseback that heralded the upheaval of Aboriginal society.

The greatest site is known as 'Major Art', a sandstone platform riddled with grottoes and daubed in paintings of all sorts: totemic figures, the innards of humans, fish bones, a Makassan sailing ketch. Several grinding holes are scoured into the rock and the skulls of ancestors are tucked into crevices, to act as protectors for subsequent generations. In this concealed, off-the-grid, extraordinary place, a snippet of the Aboriginal story is revealed.

| Where? | South Island, New Zealand |
|---|---|
| What? | A jurassic fossil forest, only revealed at low tide |

## CURIO BAY

IT FEELS halfway to the end of the earth. Head south from this wildly isolated spot and it's next stop Antarctica. The ocean pounds straight from the ice shelf, exploding on these rocks and whisking the wind into a savage, icy fury that makes playthings of seabirds and distorts the trees. At least, some of the trees. For there's a hidden forest that the weather can no longer bend. An ancient plantation that's faced the power of the elements for millions of years and, in its own way, survived. A Jurassic relic sunk into the seashore that the waves both hide and reveal ...

The Catlins Coast, which wraps around the southeast of New Zealand's South Island, is the end of the road; here, at around 46 degrees below the equator, Slope Point – the mainland's southernmost extent – is lashed by the take-no-prisoners Southern Ocean. Rugged and rocky, incised by blowholes and sea caves, flecked with reefs and river mouths, often stuck beneath sulky skies, the Catlins has an enduring wildness, as if Mother Nature is hinting that's it's not really suitable for human habitation; that survival here is going to be hard. But not so. The Maori have inhabited this far-south enclave since around AD 1350 and found it to be a natural larder. On foot, and aboard their *waka* (canoes), they discovered a shoreline rich in *kai moana* (seafood), gorging on fish, cockles, clams and seals. The rivers writhed with eels and lamprey; the forests were full of edible roots and birds, including moa and flightless kiwi. The Maori would travel widely, for food, trade and fun, setting up seasonal bases, indicated now by the remains of their middens – one such camp was at the small town

of Waikawa, where the harbour mouth and spit are home to Maori archaeological remains.

But how might these Maori have found the place 180 million years ago? For just along the coast from Waikawa – about an hour's steady walk away – is half hidden evidence of a time long before these seafarers stepped ashore, of a landscape that existed when the dinosaurs roamed. A small sweep of steep, craggy cliffs, jagged reefs and powerful seas hemmed in by headlands, Curio Bay features one of the most extensive and intact examples of a Jurassic fossil forest in the world.

During this ancient epoch, this area was at the eastern edge of the Gondwana super-continent. Back then it was a broad, tree-cloaked coastal floodplain flush with ferns, cycads, conifers and other trees similar to present-day species such as matai, kauri and Norfolk pine. It's thought a cataclysmic slide of volcanic debris crushed the forest, on multiple occasions, a fate that can now be read in the distinctive fossil bands written on the cliffs. In the many millennia since, silica began to impregnate the fallen wood, gradually transforming it into stone, preserving not just tree stumps and bark, but also tattooing the remnants of long-gone leaves into the stone. Fast forward to the past 10,000 years and the forest has been slowly exposed as the waves have gnawed at the clay and sandstone, reshaping the coast once more.

To see this petrified plantation you'll need to visit when the tide is low. At high tide the thumping sea and golden strands of leathery kelp conceal the time-frozen trees. But when the waves recede, many ossified logs and stumps can be seen, spread along the littoral. In places tree rings can be determined and bits of bark distinguished from inner trunks.

A short walkway leads to a viewing platform, which offers a vantage for looking without disturbing the rare remains. Also from here, the bay's other curios might be seen: maybe fur seals and Hector's dolphins frolicking in the surf or yellow-eyed hoiho – the rarest penguin species on the planet – waddling ashore to nest, unconcerned by what lies beneath their feet.

| Where? | Alberta, Canada |
| --- | --- |
| What? | The country's most photographed spot, long hidden from the world |

## SPIRIT ISLAND

THERE'S STILL a reverence to this place. A sense of worshipping at the altar of a colossal cathedral. The little islet – no more than a spinney of trees thrusting from the glassy green-blue – sits quietly in a granite-grey, ice-white, pine-fresh embrace. For centuries few knew of its existence, down an unknown lake, flanked by high peaks and hefty glaciers. The only visitors here were the 'mountain people', plus a menagerie of bears, beavers, caribou, moose, imperious eagles and wailing loons. Now crowds flock to see, eager to Instagram an icon. But perhaps some will also hear the whispers of its past ...

Calling Spirit Island 'hidden' is, in some ways, a stretch. It's not even an island, but rather a small land-tied spit, only cut off from the mainland following heavy spring rains. And it's certainly no secret, its image popularised and proliferated by Kodak, Apple and countless tourists so that it has become pictorial shorthand for the Rockies; the quintessence of Canadian wilderness. But it wasn't always that way. Until 1908, no white person had seen it at all.

Maligne Lake, on which Spirit Island sits, was long known to the Stoney-Nakoda First Nation, the original 'people of the mountains', whose oral tradition traces their forebears to the foothills of the Rockies from the beginning of time. They knew the lake as Chaba Imne (Beaver Lake); for them it was both a fishing ground and a sacred site. In Stoney-Nakoda mythology, mountains are considered to be physical manifestations of deceased ancestors. As the lake and its tiny isle are surrounded by soaring summits on three sides, it is considered auspicious indeed.

One First Nations story lends Spirit added significance. It's said that two young lovers from quarrelling tribes used to meet for assignations here. When the girl eventually confessed her romance to her father, he prohibited her from ever seeing her beau again. Broken-hearted, the boy continued to visit the island, desperately hoping to see her. He never did, and eventually died there, where his spirit remains.

At the turn of the 20th century, white explorers began venturing ever further west into Canada's formidable mountains – including Mary Schäffer Warren. Born into an affluent Philadelphia family in 1861, this city girl grew up to become an unlikely pioneer. She first visited the region with her botanist husband; after he died, she defied the gender conventions of her times and continued to explore on her own.

In the summer of 1908 Mary headed an expedition in search of a wondrous lake rumoured to lie in an isolated, untrampled valley; it was talked of by First Nations people but a mystery to everyone else. With a small crew, a pack of horses and a tattered sketch-map, crudely drawn by a local Stoney-Nakoda man called Sampson Beaver, breeches-wearing Mary set off. After several weeks on the trail, she became the first white person to set eyes on Maligne Lake.

Mary and her team paddled right down this 'string of pearls', finding it to stretch far into the mountains, its extent some 22 kilometres (14 miles) – the largest natural lake in the Canadian Rockies. The upper part of the lake, beyond the slender strait she named Sampson's Narrows, was, she said, 'a gem indeed'. Here, where Spirit Island lies, the deep-blue waters take on a greener tinge due to the glacial run-off, while the mountains seem to press right up tight.

Getting to Spirit Island is easy these days, though is still only possible by boat. Little motor cruisers putter from the dock at Maligne Lake's northern end, down the resplendent waterway, to reach the hidden island, halfway along. Here, a jetty provides a good vantage; access to the island itself is restricted. But better is to go by kayak. Paddle to Spirit in the early morning, before the tour boats arrive, before the cameras start clicking, and you feel a little like you've discovered it for yourself.

| Where? | Chicago, USA |
| --- | --- |
| What? | Prohibition jazz bar, favoured by Al Capone |

## THE GREEN MILL

TAKE A seat, in the velvet booth, the one across from the side door, at the end of the bar. Nice view from here: both entrances covered. The perfect spot. The bar is buzzing, with trombone and sax vibrating off the stage and a mixed crowd nursing Martinis. Days were when you couldn't get a drop to drink in here. Or weren't supposed to. But the Green Mill managed to operate outside the law. When booze was hidden underground, this was the place to be seen ...

If you wanted a drink in 1920s America, you had to do it on the hush-hush. Prohibition, in force from 1920 to 1933, saw a ban placed on the import, production or sale of alcoholic beverages countrywide. Its aim was to combat the destructive forces of booze. But it also drove drinking underground, spawning a whole new world of criminality. Liquor was illegally brewed and bootlegged, surreptitiously served at illicit speakeasies or sold openly at dubious 'pharmacies' that were permitted to sell whiskey for 'medicinal' use.

Some hangouts thrived during this supposedly dry time, including the Green Mill Cocktail Lounge. Located on North Broadway in Uptown, Chicago, it started life in 1907 as Pop Morse's Roadhouse, a stop-off for mourners en route to the nearby cemetery. But as the area developed into Chicago's entertainment district, Pop's evolved too. Looking to emulate Paris's legendary Moulin Rouge, in 1910 it was renamed the Green Mill. Occupying a whole block, it was an emporium of dancing girls, music and A-list appeal; Charlie Chaplin would drop by after a hard day's pratfalling at nearby Essanay Studios.

Chaplin wasn't the only famous patron. During the 1920s, the bar was beloved by the Mob, who ran the city's prohibition-flouting operations. Ruthless gangster 'Machine Gun' Jack McGurn, rumoured to be lead hitman at the notorious Saint Valentine's Day Massacre, owned a stake in the Green Mill. McGurn's boss – one Alphonse Gabriel Capone – frequented the place, always sitting in the same booth, from where he could monitor the comings and goings through both doors.

In fact, Capone owned a speakeasy in a basement across the street but preferred the Green Mill. Bribes paid to the police meant it could operate openly. The music was also a big draw: Billie Holiday, Al Jolson, Tommy Dorsey and Leon 'Bix' Beiderbecke all played here, while Capone's favourite, Joe E Lewis, was on a retainer. So the story goes, when Lewis said he was leaving for another club, McGurn's stooges slashed the singer's throat and sliced off a chunk of his tongue. Miraculously, Lewis survived, eventually returning to the Green Mill to perform as a stand-up comedian.

From the 1960s, Uptown's fortunes went south as the neighbourhood flooded with pimps, dealers and down-and-outs. The Green Mill endured – just. But it wasn't until a revival in the mid-80s, and the area's increasing gentrification, that this nightclub was put back on the Chicago map.

You can't miss the sign – golden spotlights twinkling behind the name in cursive lime neon. Look also for the windmill roundel carved into the brickwork down the street, marking the Green Mill's original heyday entrance. Inside, lights are low and moody in green and deep red-pink, and the walls are hung with art nouveau murals and photos of the mob. High-backed velvet booths hug white-linen tables – including that favoured by Capone. And no matter what day or time, there's usually live music.

The bar has no cocktail list – they say if you don't know what you're drinking, you shouldn't be drinking it. Maybe opt for a shot of Malört, Chicago's own intensely bitter liqueur. Somewhere behind the bar there's rumoured to be a hatch, through which black-market booze was brought up via hydraulic lift and via which mobsters could bolt, to make an exit through secret tunnels. Alas, these are off-limits. But sitting in a booth, surrounded by jazz, liquor and the ghosts of gangsters, something of the Prohibition spirit remains.

| Where? | Arizona, USA |
| --- | --- |

| What? | Secretive gorge, only reachable on foot, home to the remotest village |
| --- | --- |

## HAVASU CANYON

SUNSET, AND the day's last rays creep up and out from between the squeeze-belly walls, abandoning the canyon to the shadows. Raw, rugged rock turned in a switch-flick from fire-blaze red to shady maroon. The leaving of the light only emphasises the nowhere-ness of this secret hollow; the gulf between here and the rest of the world. But despite the darkness and the distance, life overflows here. In a sea of aridity, this is an oasis of plenty. Water pounds without pause, the soundtrack of the centuries, giving this ravine a special status, nurturing both the people who came here first and the modern-day outsiders who are lucky enough to secure a ticket ...

Havasu Baaja means People of the Blue-Green Waters. This Native American tribe (commonly known as the Havasupai) has long called the Grand Canyon home – for at least 1,400 years and, possibly, as long as 4,000. To them, this great, glorious gash in the Colorado Plateau is Wikatata (Rough Rim), and it was given to them by Tochopa, the legendary grandfather of humanity. They believe Tochopa showed them the canyon, told them this was where they would live and instructed them to go to the places where they found water. They consider themselves not merely the canyon's residents but its guardians.

Of all the tribal nations associated with the area – the Paiute, the Navajo, the Zuni, the Hopi – the Havasupai are the only ones who continue to live deep down here. Just about. For centuries the Havasupai had free rein across this sunburnt landscape, roaming across three million acres of the Grand Canyon's South Rim. But

when the Grand Canyon National Park was established in 1919, the Havasupai's lands were reduced to a tiny snip of their enormous ancestral home: a narrow side gorge, just 19 kilometres (12 miles) long by 8 kilometres (5 miles) wide.

Havasu Canyon has always been important to the Havasupai; one of their main myths centres on their challenging passage into it. There are many versions. One recounts how the canyon was once like a piston, constantly flinging open and pressing shut, crushing those who dared wander through. That is until two boys fired a volley of arrows at the rock, halting its contractions and permitting the Havasupai to enter. Another tells of a man entering with a log on his head, which he used to keep the walls wedged apart.

Its sides now permanently open, Havasu sits on the south side of the Colorado River, within the Grand Canyon but just outside the national park and far away from the rest of civilisation. Supai, the tribe's village – population around 650 – is one of the remotest communities in the USA. No roads reach it: the 13-kilometre (8-mile) trip, from the top of the rim to the bottom of the gorge, can only be done by foot, horse or helicopter. The US Postal Service transports all mail in and out by mule. Likewise, most food and other goods need to be slowly, painstakingly hefted in along the trail.

Havasu is not only physically difficult to reach, it's legally complicated too. Permits are required for the privilege of entering this hidden idyll; when the quota for the year is released, it sells out in minutes. Demand is high for such an exclusive canyon experience: while the Grand Canyon National Park sees almost 6.4 million visitors a year, Havasu receives around 20,000. Plus rules are strict: no liquor, drugs, weapons or pets must be brought in; rubbish should be carried out.

It's a rocky path down, dropping 670 metres (2,200 feet) into the guts of Arizona, a merciless undertaking beneath a hot desert sun. Tangerine dirt flies as hooves and hikers descend between regiments of cacti and towers of rusty rock, some weather-hewn into creatures, others looking ominously ready to fall. At Supai village, a handful of timber-frame houses lolls around a dusty plaza, pinched between the sheer sandstone. There's a café and a lodge but not much else. The beauty is just beyond.

Graceful Havasu Falls gleams and thunders amid its rock-bottom home. It's a classic cascade, plunging 35 metres (115 feet) in brilliant blue-green, given its dazzling hue by the high concentration of calcium carbonate. You can swim in the pools, duck behind the plume and explore the cracks and crevices in the cliffs. It's magnificent and vital, a postcard-perfect lifeline. The falls are fed by a limestone aquifer, which pumps year-round, irrigating the Havasupai's crop of squash, corn, beans and peaches. It is springs such as these that have enabled the tribe to survive this hostile environment for so long. More than that, this waterfall – and the chain of others that tumble through Havasu – provides a spiritual connection between the Native American people and the earth; the water, they say, speaks to them.

Since the initial allocation of land, the Havasupai have managed to reclaim more of their former homelands – though still only a fraction of the area they once traversed. Their existence is currently threatened by the development of uranium mines upstream from Supai, which they fear could cause contamination and turn the water into a poisonous stream. The Havasupai are now campaigning for a ban on mining in the area, fighting to protect their home and the very essence of Wikatata. Long after they were given this place to call home, the Havasupai remain its steadfast guardians.

What? Abolitionist hub and 'Grand Central Depot' of the Underground Railroad

## PLYMOUTH CHURCH OF THE PILGRIMS

IMAGINE HUDDLING in the pitch-black darkness for a night – maybe two – all alone in the hollows beneath this house of God. Cold, disorientated, terrified; devoid of possessions or even status as a human being. But full of hope. Because this unlit basement is no prison. It's freedom. In the bright and brimful auditorium up above, the world is being put to rights. Voices are crying for the liberty of those so long kept in the shadows ...

The Underground Railroad was a dangerous ride. Borrowing terminology from the real railways starting to spread across the USA, this notional version – at its busiest from around 1830 to 1865 – was the clandestine network of ordinary people whose houses provided refuge to slaves fleeing the American South. It had many 'tracks' (routes) and 'stations' (hiding places). 'Conductors' aided the 'cargo' (escaped slaves). Reaching the 'terminal' meant making it to the northern states and Canada – to freedom.

One key stop on this risky journey was the Plymouth Church of the Pilgrims. This stout red-brick in Brooklyn Heights was built in 1849. By then the borough was booming, with the bustling docks of the East River providing enough distraction for smuggling in fugitive slaves; they'd be bundled off boats and snuck up the hill to the safety of the church, only a few blocks away. Brooklyn was also a hotbed of abolitionist sentiment, thanks in no small part to the fiery, theatrical oratory of Henry Ward Beecher, the first preacher of Plymouth Church. Beecher was a rock star of religion. His sermons were packed with worshippers from near and far; the Sunday morning Brooklyn ferries became known as 'Beecher boats'

because they were crammed with people coming purely to hear him speak. And what he spoke of was the ending of slavery. Beecher, like his sister – author Harriet Beecher Stowe – was a passionate abolitionist and a voice of the national conscience. 'Liberty,' he wrote, 'is the soul's right to breathe and, when it cannot take a long breath, laws are girdled too tight.'

He was also a 'stationmaster', helping untold amounts of cargo find its way to freedom. 'I opened Plymouth Church, though you did not know it, to hide fugitives,' he once claimed. 'I took them into my own home and fed them. I piloted them, and sent them toward the North Star, which to them was the Star of Bethlehem.' This was a risky business. A slave was deemed the property of its master, so helping such property escape was considered theft. But Beecher was undeterred, and his church became known as the Underground Railroad's Grand Central Depot.

Henry Ward Beecher can still be found in his parish. His statue stands in the church garden, next to a bas-relief of Abraham Lincoln, both of which were sculpted by Mount Rushmore artist Gutzon Borglum; in an unsavoury twist, Borglum was a member of the Ku Klux Klan. Inside, and befitting Beecher's style, the white-walled nave feels more theatre than church, with ground-floor pews and upper balcony curving like stalls and dress circle before a stage. One of those pews – number 89, in the fourth row – is where Lincoln sat when he visited on 26 February 1860. The day after he gave his famous anti-slavery speech in Manhattan; that November he was elected President.

However, the church's most moving story lies behind the pulpit and the pipe organ, where a nondescript door reveals a secret staircase. On a special tour you can descend into the vaults, tread the bare-dirt floors and red-brick passageways, stoop under the arches to enter the maze of chambers, smell the cold, earthy air. You can even feel the absolute darkness when the lights are switched off and wonder how it must have felt when a night spent here was your best option; a frightening step on the journey to freedom.

Where? Cayo District, Belize

What? Jungle-shrouded cave,
purported gateway to
the Maya underworld

## ACTUN TUNICHIL MUKNAL

THE NARROW cave entrance bulges top and bottom like an hourglass, a slender slot both in the jungle-draped limestone and, so it seems, in time itself. This spot, deep in the Maya Mountains, tucked amid the cohune palms and ceiba trees, cut off by rivers, over-swung by monkeys and stalked by jaguars, already feels far removed from the 21st century. Now, to delve deeper still. To wade into the cool, blue pool at the cave mouth, to feel tiny fish nibbling bare skin, to hear splashes echoing off the shadowy walls, to leave behind the last shafts of cheering sunlight for an altogether darker realm. Ahead is the unremitting blackness of the earth's belly, with just pinpricks of torchlight to illuminate the strange rock formations, the shards of broken earthenware and, yes, the sparkling human bones. This is the place where the living and the dead collide for reasons not quite known ...

Central America is riddled with caves, caverns and plunging cenotes (sinkholes). Millennia of sea-level changes and rain erosion have gnawed at the region's bedrock of porous limestone, sculpting it into a geological Swiss cheese. Fascinating for speleologists. Terrifying and irresistible for the ancient Maya.

Since around 2000 BC, various Maya groups have roamed the hole-pocked terrain of what are now Guatemala, Mexico and Belize. Subsequently, cave motifs crop up repeatedly in their culture: they are painted on vases, etched onto stelae, mentioned in songs and stories. For the Maya, Tlaltícpac was the surface of the earth and the gaps in it – the caves and cenotes – were entrances to Xibalbá, the underworld: a multi-level Place of Fear, ruled by a

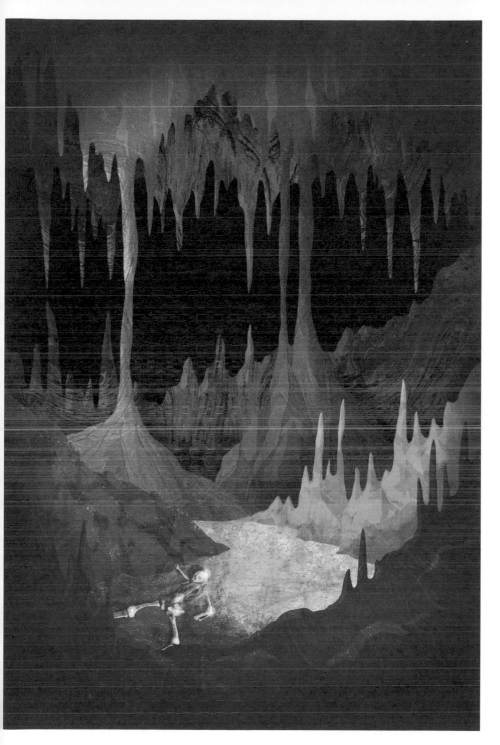

cohort of malign, ultra-violent gods with bone-chilling names such as One Death and Seven Death, Pus Master, Skull Sceptre and Bloody Claws. The Popol Vuh, the Maya creation story, tells of Hero Twins Hunahpu and Xbalanque descending to Xibalbá to fight these nefarious forces; after being imprisoned with bats, big cats, extreme cold and raging fires, the duo manages to beat the gods at a ball game and ultimately slaughter many of the demons before using a canoe to return to the land of the living. They are the only beings ever to escape that wretched place.

Hidden within central Belize's Tapir Mountain Nature Reserve, Actun Tunichil Muknal (the Cave of the Stone Sepulchre) is purportedly one such gateway to the underworld. Only discovered in 1989, and opened to the intrepid public in 1998, it is thought to have been visited frequently by the Maya during the Classic period, from around AD 250 to 900, when great cities such as Copán and Tikal were flourishing. The Maya utilised caves for various functions: larders, hideaways, water sources and ceremonial sites. Actun Tunichil Muknal appears to have been the latter.

As well as being doorways to hell, caves were also considered the origin of the most essential resource. Chaac, god of rain, was thought to reside on the fringes of Xibalbá, and his watery beneficence was believed to issue from these fissures in the rocky crust.

Offerings dating from the Classic era, including snail shells, ceramic pots and pieces of obsidian, have been discovered at Actun Tunichil Muknal. Items found around the cave's entrance date from across the entire period, but those deeper inside the system can be traced exclusively to the eighth and ninth centuries. For that brief period, something compelled those ancient peoples to take the risk and venture deeper into the underworld. And when they did so, they were not just leaving jars and stones, they were making human sacrifices. Shortly after this time, the Maya civilisation collapsed. No one knows exactly why but it's posited that a severe drought ravaged Central America, causing the population to plummet and, perhaps, causing the desperate Maya to make more and more valuable offerings to Chaac and the demons of the deep.

Today, getting to Actun Tunichil Muknal is scarcely any less arduous than it must have been 1,000 years ago. Tours are guided, but a sense of adventure is still required. First, there's a trek through damp, snake-slithered, mist-hung jungle. It's about an hour's hike, via waist-deep rivers, tangled roots, cliff niches, ancient artefacts and foliage alive with creatures: prolific butterflies and birds, maybe a coatimundi scurrying amid the trees; a jaguar sighting would be rare indeed.

At the cave mouth, there's no choice but to sink into the chill turquoise pool and paddle through the slit into the entrance cavern. What follows is pure Indiana Jones: part-swim, part-hike, part-clamber. You'll pass cat-shaped stalactites and rocks a-glitter with crystal flows. You'll haul onto rock shelves, step carefully amid ancient *ollas* (jars) and slabs carved to represent blood-letting tools, hoping not to disturb the whip spiders. You'll enter the 'Cathedral', a soaring-ceilinged space of stalagmites and calcite curtains. And you'll duck down narrow passageways seemingly designed by the demons themselves.

In the farthest, blackest recesses of Actun Tunichil Muknal lie the bones. Around 14 skeletons have been discovered, ranging in age from infant to adult. Most appear to have been killed by blunt trauma to the head. Some are tucked into small caves and cracks; others lie spread in the open.

Most macabre and magnificent of all is the 'Crystal Maiden', an intact skeleton – thought to be an 18-year-old girl – from a human sacrifice made over 1,000 years ago. Now, she lies in the dust, her bones encrusted with calcite crystals, formed by the deposition of minerals over the years. They make her inert frame sparkle in the torchlight. An unfortunate victim ritually despatched to bring a glimmer of hope to a doomed civilisation, now bringing a glimmer of horror and history to this dark, mysterious place.

Where?   Cusco Region, Peru

What?   Majestic, mountain-spilled
Inca city, only accessible
on foot

## CHOQUEQUIRAO

MIST SWIRLS through the Apurímac valley, lacing the forested slopes, variously obscuring and then revealing the snow-capped peaks above. There's something else amid the clouds too, something simultaneously out of place in this wild, natural scene yet also built in harmony with its contours. The lost city of Choquequirao – in local Quechua, the 'cradle of gold'. Neat terraces of Inca stonework tumble down the mountainsides, sprawl across hilltops, tuck into grooves; walls and ruins stand clear from the grass. But more – much more – of this remote citadel lies still smothered in the jungle, it secrets still hidden from view ...

Peru's famed 'lost city' is Machu Picchu, the Andes-clinging Incan stronghold only rediscovered in 1911 and now visited by over one million people a year. But just across the mountains, about 40 kilometres (25 miles) as the condor flies, is another Inca site, spread across multiple slopes, far larger than Machu Picchu, which sees fewer than 6,000 annual visitors.

Choquequirao was built in the late 15th century, at the apogee of the Inca empire, at around the same time as Machu Picchu. The two are considered sister sites: both comprise a collection of stone buildings arranged around a plaza, along astronomical alignments, located on steep ridges above a raging river, surrounded by the breath-stealing peaks that the Inca believed to be *apus* – mountain gods, the protectors of the people.

The Spanish explorer Juan Arias Díaz found Choquequirao in 1710; in 1909 American academic Hiram Bingham stopped by the ruins before going on to reveal Machu Picchu to the world two

years later. However, while archaeological excavations began at Machu Picchu almost as soon as it was found, Choquequirao – thanks to its scale and tough-to-access location, 3,000 metres (9,842 feet) above sea level – was left largely untouched until the 1970s; even now, only around 40 per cent has been excavated.

The city's precise purpose remains unknown. It may have been a royal residence, an agricultural hub for the cultivation of coca leaves, a pilgrimage or religious site, or an entry point into Willkapampa, the final refuge of the Inca Empire until it fell to the Spanish in 1572. It may have been all of these things. One thing is certain: Choquequirao, with its fine buildings and road links to other sites, was important indeed.

The site is not well connected these days, however. Currently, the only way to reach Choquequirao is via a strenuous two-day trek from the backwater village of Cachora. Strenuous because it requires a knee-jarring descent into a near mile-deep canyon and an even steeper, higher climb up the other side in a series of thigh-burning switchbacks. Even with the help of kit-carrying mules and hot coca tea (to help stave off altitude sickness), it's a challenge. Which keeps it relatively tourist free, and all the more atmospheric.

The Inca believed in the duality of life – similar to Chinese yin and yang – and the design of Choquequirao observed this balance, separated into *hanan* (higher) and *hurin* (lower) sectors. A stone canal connects the two, feeding the water of the gods from the Hanan Square – the site's loftiest part – to the Main Square below. Built into the hillsides around are impressive feats of stonework: large *collcas* (storehouses), long *lkallankas* (priests' houses), a set of 16 irrigated ceremonial platforms aligned to the winter solstice. There are also temples, fountains, ritual baths, workshops, kitchens and *kanchas* (holding pens) for llamas, which were sacrificed in certain ceremonies. These animals appear again on the western slopes, where a set of cascading terraces features camelid figures made of carved white rock.

There is talk of improving the infrastructure, to make it easier to reach Choquequirao; a cable car has been signed off by the Peruvian government, and construction is due to start imminently. Allegedly. But for now, the mountains remain quiet, offbeat and isolated. An example of Inca mastery, far from the masses.

Where? Péten, Guatemala

What? Vast Maya citadel,
swallowed by the jungle

## EL MIRADOR

IT'S HOT – steaming hot. The air heavy enough to slice. Sweat streaming in rivulets. Insects humming. Howler monkeys earning their name. The jungle rears higher, a looming canopy of mahogany, cedar and spiny ceiba, Guatemala's national tree which was considered sacred by the ancient Maya, who believed its roots grew down into the underworld. Seems appropriate. For this particular patch of forest hides one of the Maya's largest, earliest and most astonishing cities. A place that's lain abandoned for centuries and is only now beginning to reveal its secrets ...

The Maya civilisation spanned from around 2000 BC to AD 900 – though there are still modern Maya people living across Central America today. During their era of dominance, the Maya founded powerful settlements featuring large plazas, exquisite stone carvings and enormous stepped pyramids. Many visitors converge on the Guatemalan site of Tikal – once an important capital – to appreciate Mayan architectural virtuosity at its best restored and most reachable.

However, secreted away in the country's remote, wild, densely tangled Petén region in the far north, is a city that was bigger and grander than better-known Tikal, yet is now visited by only a handful of people. El Mirador's heyday was from around 300 BC to AD 150, during the Mayan Preclassic period, well before Tikal came to prominence some 500 years later. Spread across a series of low, limestone hills, El Mirador was twice the size of Tikal, with a purported population of over 80,000 people.

For reasons unknown – perhaps environmental degradation or threats from nearby rivals such as Teotihuacán in Mexico –

El Mirador collapsed. It was rediscovered in 1926, and aerial photographs taken in 1930 revealed its massive peaks of man-made stone protruding from the rainforest canopy. And that's largely how El Mirador remains. An overgrown behemoth, still consumed by nature.

Only a fraction of the 16-square kilometre (6-square mile) site has been excavated, partly because the vegetation helps protect the ruins from the damaging effects of the sun, partly because it's such a Sisyphean task.

Unless you're in possession of a helicopter, the only way to get to El Mirador is on foot or by mule from the village of Carmelita. It takes two days, on a route that becomes a knee-deep mud bath during the rainy season, and remains a broiling, buggy expedition year round, with the possibility of meeting deadly fer-de-lance snakes, toxic chechen trees or even jaguar.

But it's worth it. The grand scale and sophistication of El Mirador is still evident even beneath its thick green cloak. Not least the triadic pyramid of La Danta, which at 70 metres (230 feet) is the tallest the Maya ever built; researchers estimate it would have taken 15 million man-days to construct. Today, wooden ladders lead up La Danta's steep, stepped flank to the summit, from where the tops of the site's other pyramids jut up above the rampant trees.

Rising 55 metres (180 feet) high, El Tigre is the site's second largest complex and faces La Danta on an east–west axis. Its Jaguar Paw Temple has been well excavated, revealing panels depicting Maya deities and big cats. Between these pyramids lies the Central Acropolis, a plaza where coronations and sacrifices would have been performed. Here, the carved stucco of the Central Acropolis frieze show Hunahpu and Xbalanque, the Hero Twins of Maya creation mythology, carrying their father's severed head through the underworld.

But El Mirador's reach extended far further into the jungle. The city was the ceremonial nexus of many interconnected settlements, encompassing maybe a million people. A network of *sacbeob*, chalky-white limestone causeways, ran across the Mirador Basin, linking these settlements together. Follow this road system today and you'll find countless Mayan ruins, including the huge city of El Tintal (second only in size to El Mirador) and the older temples at Nakbé. Impressive sites, long hidden. Which make you wonder, what else might be concealed within this impenetrable sea of green?

SARAH BAXTER grew up in Norfolk, England and now lives in Bath. Her passion for travel and the great outdoors saw her traverse Asia, Australia, New Zealand and the United States before settling into a writing career.

She was Associate Editor of *Wanderlust* magazine, the bible for independent-minded travellers, for more than ten years and has also written extensively on travel for a diverse range of other publications, including the *Guardian*, the *Telegraph* and the *Independent* newspapers. Sarah has contributed to more than a dozen Lonely Planet guidebooks and is the author of the first two books in the *Inspired Traveller's Guide* series, *Spiritual Places* and *Literary Places*, as well as *A History of the World in 500 Walks* and *A History of the World in 500 Railway Journeys*.

AMY GRIMES is an illustrator based in London. Drawing inspiration from nature and the natural world, Amy's work often features bright and bold illustrated motifs, floral icons and leafy landscapes. As well as working on commissioned illustrations, Amy also sells prints under the brand of Hello Grimes.